SHEPHERD'S NOTES

Shepherd's Notes Titles Available

SHEPHERD'S NOTES COMMENTARY SERIES

Old Testament

0-80549-028-0	Genesis	0-80549-341-7	Psalms 101-150
0-80549-056-6	Exodus	0-80549-016-7	Proverbs
0-80549-069-8	Leviticus & Numbers	0-80549-059-0	Ecclesiastes, Song of Solomon
0-80549-027-2	Deuteronomy		
0-80549-058-2	Joshua & Judges	0-80549-197-X	Isaiah
0-80549-057-4	Ruth & Esther	0-80549-070-1	Jeremiah-Lamentations
0-80549-063-9	1 & 2 Samuel		
0-80549-007-8	1 & 2 Kings	0-80549-078-7	Ezekiel
0-80549-064-7	1 & 2 Chronicles	0-80549-015-9	Daniel
0-80549-194-5	Ezra, Nehemiah	0-80549-326-3	Hosea-Obadiah
0-80549-006-X	Job	0-80549-334-4	Jonah-Zephaniah
0-80549-339-5	Psalms 1-50	0-80549-065-5	Haggai-Malachi
0-80549-340-9	Psalms 51-100		

New Testament

1-55819-688-9	Matthew	1-55819-689-7	Philippians, Colossians, & Philemon
0-80549-071-X	Mark		
0-80549-004-3	Luke		
1-55819-693-5	John	0-80549-000-0	1 & 2 Thessalonians
1-55819-691-9	Acts	1-55819-692-7	1 & 2 Timothy, Titus
0-80549-005-1	Romans	0-80549-336-0	Hebrews
0-80549-325-5	1 Corinthians	0-80549-018-3	James
0-80549-335-2	2 Corinthians	0-80549-019-1	1 & 2 Peter & Jude
1-55819-690-0	Galatians	0-80549-214-3	1, 2 & 3 John
0-80549-327-1	Ephesians	0-80549-017-5	Revelation

SHEPHERD'S NOTES CHRISTIAN CLASSICS

0-80549-347-6	Mere Christianity-C.S.Lewis	0-80549-394-8	Miracles-C.S.Lewis
0-80549-353-0	The Problem of Pain/ A Grief Observed-C.S.Lewis	0-80549-196-1	Lectures to My Students-Charles Haddon Spurgeon
0-80549-199-6	The Confessions-Augustine	0-80549-220-8	The Writings of Justin Martyr
0-80549-200-3	Calvin's Institutes	0-80549-345-X	The City of God

SHEPHERD'S NOTES-BIBLE SUMMARY SERIES

0-80549-377-8	Old Testament	0-80549-385-9	Life & Letters of Paul
0-80549-378-6	New Testament	0-80549-376-X	Manners & Customs of Bible Times
0-80549-384-0	Life & Teachings of Jesus	0-80549-380-8	Basic Christian Beliefs

SHEPHERD'S NOTES

When you need a guide through the Scriptures

Mark

HOLMAN REFERENCE

Nashville, Tennessee

Shepherd's Notes®—*Mark*
© 1999
by Broadman & Holman Publishers
Nashville, Tennessee
All rights reserved
Printed in the United States of America

0–8054–9071–X
Dewey Decimal Classification: 22.3
Subject Heading: BIBLE. N.T. Mark
Library of Congress Card Catalog Number: 99–11542

Library of Congress Cataloging-in-Publication Data
Gould, Dana, 1951–
Mark / Dana Gould, editor [i.e. author].
        p. cm. — (Shepherd's notes)
    Includes bibliographical references.
    ISBN 0–8054–9071–X
    1. Bible. N.T. Mark—Study and teaching.   I. Title.   II. Series
BS2585.4.B58   1999
226.3'07—dc21   99–11542
                                                                                CIP

3 4 5 6   08 07 06 05

CONTENTS

FOREWORD

Dear Reader:

Shepherd's Notes are designed to give you a quick, step-by-step overview of every book of the Bible. They are not meant to be substitutes for the biblical text; rather, they are study guides intended to help you explore the wisdom of Scripture in personal or group study and to apply that wisdom successfully in your own life.

Shepherd's Notes guide you through the main themes of each book of the Bible and illuminate fascinating details through appropriate commentary and reference notes. Historical and cultural background information brings the Bible into sharper focus.

Six different icons, used throughout the series, call your attention to historical-cultural information, Old Testament and New Testament references, word pictures, unit summaries, and personal application for everyday life.

Whether you are a novice or a veteran at Bible study, I believe you will find *Shepherd's Notes* a resource that will take you to a new level in your mining and applying the riches of Scripture.

In Him,

David R. Shepherd
Editor-in-Chief

DESIGNED FOR THE BUSY USER

Shepherd's Notes for the Gospel of Mark is designed to provide an easy-to-use tool for getting a quick handle on this Bible book's important features, and for gaining an understanding of the message of Mark. Information available in more difficult-to-use reference works has been incorporated into the *Shepherd's Notes* format. This brings you the benefits of many more advanced and expensive works packed into one small volume.

Shepherd's Notes are for laymen, pastors, teachers, small group leaders and participants, as well as the classroom student. Enrich your personal study or quiet time. Shorten your class or small group preparation time as you gain valuable insights into the truths of God's Word that you can pass along to your students or group members.

DESIGNED FOR QUICK ACCESS

Bible students with time constraints will especially appreciate the time-saving features built in the *Shepherd's Notes*. All features are intended to aid a quick and concise encounter with the heart of the message.

Concise Commentary. Mark is replete with characters, places, events, and instruction to believers. Short sections provide quick "snapshots" of sections, highlighting important points and other information.

Outlined Text. A comprehensive outline covers the entire text of Mark. This is a valuable feature for following the narrative's flow, allowing for a quick, easy way to locate a particular passage.

Shepherd's Notes. These summary statements appear at the close of every key section of the narrative. While functioning in part as a quick summary, they also deliver the essence of the message presented in the sections they cover.

Icons. Various icons in the margin highlight recurring themes in Mark and aid in selective searching or tracing of those themes.

Sidebars and Charts. These specially selected features provide additional background information to your study or preparation. These include definitions as well as cultural, historical, and biblical insights.

Maps. These are placed at appropriate places in the book to aid your understanding and study of a text or passage.

Questions to Guide Your Study. These thought-provoking questions and discussion starters are designed to encourage interaction with the truths and principles of God's Word.

In addition to the above features, study aids have been included at the back of the book for those readers who require or desire more information and resources for working through Mark's narrative. These include chapter outlines for studying Mark and a list of reference sources used for this volume which offer many works that allow the reader to extend the scope of his or her study of Mark.

DESIGNED TO WORK FOR YOU

Personal Study. Using the *Shepherd's Notes* with a passage of Scripture can enlighten your study and take it a new level. At your fingertips is information that would require searching several volumes to find. In addition, many points of application occur throughout the volume, contributing to personal growth.

Teaching. Outlines frame the text of Mark and provide a logical presentation of the message. Shepherd's Notes provide summary statements for presenting the essence of key points and events. Personal Application icons point out personal application of the message in Mark's Gospel, and Historical Context icons indicate where background information is supplied.

Group Study. Shepherd's Notes can be an excellent companion volume to use for gaining a quick but accurate understanding of the message of a Bible book. Each group member can benefit by having his or her own copy. The *Note's* format accommodates the study of or the tracing of the themes throughout Mark. Leaders may use its flexible features to prepare for group sessions, or use during group sessions. Questions to Guide Your Study can spark discussion of the key points and truths of Mark's Gospel.

LIST OF MARGIN ICONS USED IN MARK

 Shepherd's Notes. Placed at the end of each section, a capsule statement provides the reader with the essence of the message of that section.

 Historical Context. To indicate historical information—historical, biographical, cultural—and provide insight on the understanding or interpretation of a passage.

 Old Testament Reference. Used when the writer refers to Old Testament passages or when Old Testament passages illuminate a text.

 New Testament Reference. Used when the writer refers to New Testament passages that are either fulfilled prophecy, an antitype of an Old Testament type, or a New Testament text which in some other way illuminates the passages under discussion.

 Personal Application. Used when the text provides a personal or universal application of truth.

 Word Picture. Indicates that the meaning of a specific word or phrase is illustrated so as to shed light on it.

INTRODUCTION

The Gospel of Mark is the shortest of the four accounts of the life and teaching of Jesus. Many scholars believe it was the first Gospel written.

Gospel of Mark in a "Nutshell"

PURPOSE:	To preserve the story of Jesus after the passing of first-generation Christians
THEME:	Kingdom of God
MAJOR DOCTRINE:	Discipleship
OTHER DOCTRINES:	Doctrine of Christ, Doctrine of the Last Days

Papias, bishop of Hierapolis, who lived from about A.D. 60 to 130, is one of the earliest sources to mention the Gospel of Mark. Eusebius quoted Papias: "Mark was the interpreter of Peter and wrote accurately but not in order of whatever he remembered about the things which were said or done by the Lord" (Quoted in *Church History* 3.39.15).

AUTHOR

The title "according to Mark" was added to this Gospel by scribes who produced the earliest copies of the Gospel. According to early church tradition, Mark recorded and arranged the "memories" of Peter, thereby producing a Gospel based on apostolic witness. Peter was undoubtedly the source for most of Mark's Gospel. Besides the content that came from Peter, there is indication of Mark's own narrative and the inclusion of gospel truths that had been spoken by others and now were being put into writing. Mark himself may have been an eyewitness to part of what he wrote. Regardless of his sources, the Holy Spirit used Mark's own personality in the writing.

Although Mark was a common Roman name, the Gospel writer was probably John Mark.

Mark became an important assistant for both Paul and Peter, preaching the Good News to

Gentiles and preserving the gospel message for later Christians. Some traditions maintain that Mark died a martyr's death.

AUDIENCE

Mark wrote his Gospel for Gentile Christians. He explained Jewish customs in detail for the benefit of readers unfamiliar with Judaism (7:3–4; 12:18). Mark translated several Aramaic expressions for a Greek-speaking audience (5:41; 7:11, 34; 15:22). Gentiles would have especially appreciated Mark's interpretation of the saying of Jesus which declared all foods clean (7:19; cp. with Matt. 15:17–20). Mark's Gentile audience may explain his omission of the genealogy of Jesus. Perhaps these Gentile readers were Roman Christians.

Mark's Gospel contains many terms borrowed from Latin and written in Greek, including "taking counsel" (3:6), "Legion" (5:9), "tribute" (12:14), and "flogged" (15:15).

Early Christian tradition places Mark in Rome preserving the words of Peter for Roman Christians shortly before the apostle's death (see 1 Pet. 5:13). According to tradition, Peter was martyred in Rome during the Neronian persecution, which would place the date of Mark's Gospel about A.D. 64 to 68. Such a hostile environment motivated Mark to couch his account of the life of Jesus in terms that would comfort Christians suffering for their faith. The theme of persecution dominates the Gospel of Mark (10:30; cp. Matt. 19:29; Luke 18:29). Jesus' messianic suffering is emphasized to inspire Christians to follow the same path of servanthood (10:42–45). Roman Christians would be encouraged, knowing that Jesus anticipated that "everyone will be salted with fire" (9:49; 13:9–13). Dying for the gospel would be equivalent to dying for Jesus (8:35; Matt. 16:25; Luke 9:24).

PURPOSE FOR WRITING

The concerns Mark addressed were typical of Christians of his generation and are pertinent to ours. Mark wrote to preserve the story of Jesus after the deaths of first-generation Christians such as Peter. Mark, however, was not a mere archivist, for he used the story of Jesus for pastoral purposes.

1. Mark wrote to encourage Christians to persist in faithful discipleship, particularly in the crisis of persecution. Sometimes Mark used Jesus' sayings to encourage perseverance (8:34–38; 13:11). More often he encouraged faithful discipleship through the examples of his characters: Jesus, who by His exorcisms and healings triumphed over evil but who committed Himself to a life of humble service, suffering, and death. John the Baptizer, who was Jesus' forerunner in proclamation and death. Those first disciples, who left all to follow Jesus but who often lacked faith and understanding and who failed Jesus through their rebuke, betrayal, denial, and abandonment. The women, who anointed Jesus for His death, who accepted the suffering, dying Christ of the cross and tomb. Bartimaeus, who once was blind but then through the mercy of the Son of David saw and followed Jesus in the way of the cross.

2. Mark encouraged Christians to courageous witness. The call of the first disciples included Jesus' promise to make them "fishers of men" (1:17; cp. 6:6b–13). Mark encouraged witness in the face of Jewish opposition through the

The oldest manuscripts of Mark end with the fear and silence of the women in 16:8. This puzzling ending reminds contemporary disciples that the Jesus story is unfinished until we share the message boldly with our generation.

thirteen "conflict stories" illustrating Jesus' authority (2:1–3:6; 3:20–35; 7:1–23; 10:1–12; 11:27–12:37). Mark likewise encouraged witness through the example of his characters: the friends of the paralytic who brought him to Jesus; the former demoniac who proclaimed how much Jesus had done for him; the Syrophoenician women who envisioned a gospel that reached the Gentiles; the people of Bethsaida who brought a blind man to Jesus for healing; those who brought their "little ones" to Jesus; and ultimately Jesus before the Sanhedrin (14:62; see 13:11).

3. Mark encouraged Christians to hope in the promises of Jesus. Mark might be termed "the Gospel of loose ends." Mark often pointed ahead to promises that were only fulfilled *outside* his story. For example, John promised one who "will baptize . . . with the Holy Spirit" (1:8); Jesus promised that God's "mustard seed" of a kingdom would become a "large" plant (4:30–32), and that disciples would be given grace to share Jesus' cup of suffering and baptism of death (10:39). Also John promised that the Spirit would enable disciples to withstand persecution and witness boldly (13:9–13) and that Jesus would meet His disciples in Galilee after the resurrection (14:28; 16:7). Mark doubtless knew traditions such as those Luke incorporated in Acts that related the fulfillment of such promises.

That Mark left these "loose ends" suggests that for Mark the "Jesus story" is not finished until it is finished through the bold witness and costly discipleship of His followers.

DATE OF WRITING

Precisely how early Mark wrote his Gospel is not certain, but some leading scholars hold that A.D. 50 is quite probable (A. T. Robertson, *Word Pictures in the New Testament*, "Matthew and Mark" vol. 1, 249).

THE PLACE OF MARK'S GOSPEL

The Gospel of Mark was more or less treated as the stepchild of the Gospels until relatively recent times. When it became widely held that Mark was the first and primary Gospel, it was then moved front and center of attention. Matthew and Luke had obviously had great appreciation for Mark from the very beginning.

LITERARY STYLE

Good storytellers captivate audiences by using everyday language that provokes strong imagery. Mark's language is simple, direct, and understandable.

LITERARY FORM

Upon first reading, the Gospel of Mark appears to be an arbitrary collection of stories about Jesus. However, upon closer inspection, it becomes apparent to the observant reader that Mark arranges the material in a more sophisticated fashion to convey truth on a higher level.

Mark tells the story of Jesus as a whole. Mark develops the unifying "plot" of the gospel story by unveiling the hidden identity of Jesus. The messianic secret is part of the mystery of the kingdom of God, understood only by insiders—"to those on the outside everything is said in parables" (4:11, 33–34). Mark uses the messianic secret to organize his story around the progressive revelation of Christ and the faith pilgrimage of His disciples.

Matthew has the essence of more than 90 percent of Mark's verses, and Luke has the essence of more than 50 percent of Mark's verses. The two Gospels often use Mark's actual words as they see things together with Mark. (Matthew, Mark, and Luke are known as the Synoptic Gospels, which means "to see together.") Only one-third of Mark's verses do not appear somewhere in Matthew or Luke. John's Gospel may well have benefitted from acquaintance with Mark.

The literary form of Mark's Gospel is no accident. The arrangement of the Gospel material gives every indication that a skilled literary craftsman has been at work.

QUESTIONS TO GUIDE YOUR STUDY

1. What did Mark wish to accomplish with his Gospel?
2. What features distinguish Mark's Gospel account from Matthew, Luke, and John?
3. What are the key themes of Mark's Gospel?
4. Based on this introduction, what are we to gain from a study of Mark's Gospel?

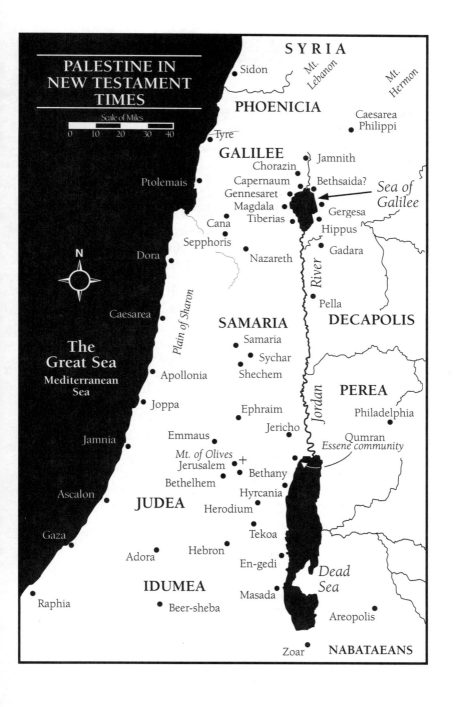

PALESTINE IN NEW TESTAMENT TIMES

Scale of Miles
0   10   20   30   40

SYRIA

Sidon

Mt. Lebanon

Mt. Hermon

PHOENICIA

Caesarea Philippi

Tyre

GALILEE

Chorazin   Jamnith

Capernaum   Bethsaida?

Ptolemais   Gennesaret

Magdala   *Sea of Galilee*

Cana   Tiberias   Gergesa

Sepphoris   Hippus

Dora   Gadara

Nazareth

River

Caesarea   Pella

SAMARIA   **DECAPOLIS**

Plain of Sharon   Samaria

The Great Sea   Sychar

Mediterranean Sea Shechem

Apollonia   **PEREA**

Jordan

Joppa   Ephraim   Philadelphia

Jamnia   Jericho

Emmaus   Qumran
                   Essene community

Mt. of Olives

Jerusalem   Bethany

Bethlehem

Ascalon   Hyrcania

JUDEA   Herodium

Gaza   Tekoa

Adora   Hebron

En-gedi   *Dead Sea*

IDUMEA   Masada

Raphia   Beer-sheba

Areopolis

Zoar   **NABATAEANS**

The word *gospel* refers to the announcement of the good news, not its prediction. To this point, the gospel had been anticipated; now it becomes a present event.

Mark begins his account by focusing on the source and content of the good news of Jesus Christ. He then gives attention to Jesus' baptism and wilderness temptation before moving on to begin his story of Jesus' ministry.

THE BEGINNING OF THE GOOD NEWS (1:1)

Mark's first verse offers the theme and summary of the book. "Beginning of the gospel" sums up the entire book and its events.

The source of the good news: Jesus Christ. *Jesus* was a common Hebrew name equivalent to *Joshua,* which means "Yahweh saves." Christ was the Greek translation for the Hebrew word that means "messiah" or "anointed one."

Mark completes the title of his book with the term "Son of God," which points to Jesus' divinity.

ANNOUNCING THE GOOD NEWS (1:2–3)

Mark begins his story with the God-inspired promise of the prophets Malachi and Isaiah (cp. Mal. 3:1 and Isa. 40:3 with Mark 1:2–3).

PICTURING THE GOOD NEWS IN SYMBOL (1:4–5)

When John the Baptist appears as the appointed messenger, his work is laid out for him. He is to make a road for the Lord, use preaching as his method, and tell people to prepare themselves for the Lord's coming.

When a king traveled in those days, he sent workers to smooth the road and announce his coming. That was John's job for the King of kings.

According to Luke's Gospel, John the Baptist began his ministry around the Jordan River in the fifteenth year of the reign of Tiberias Caesar (Luke 3:1–3), which must have been A.D. 26 or 27. John's preaching emphasized the coming judgment, the need for repentance, and the coming of the Messiah. He lived an austere existence. He wore the dress of a prophet—camel's hair and a leather belt (Matt. 3:4; Mark 1:6). He was beheaded by Herod Antipas.

John preached a message of repentance. He baptized those people who repented in the Jordan River.

Verse 5, "The whole Judean countryside and all the people of Jerusalem went out to him," means that all kinds of people, in great numbers, came to John for baptism.

FULFILLING PROPHECY (1:6–8)
John the Baptist further fulfilled prophecy by arriving on the scene like an Old Testament prophet. John's food was locusts and wild honey.

John drew a sharp contrast between his water baptism and Jesus' Holy Spirit baptism. John's water immersion was momentary, and it pictured the purified life of repentance. Jesus' Holy Spirit immersion will be eternal in nature, and it will actually purify. Jesus will saturate His followers with His Holy Spirit.

Repentance

In the New Testament, the word *repentance* means "coming to one's senses; a change of mind that shows up in a person's life through his beliefs, commitments, attitudes, and behavior."

THE BAPTISM AND TEMPTATION OF JESUS (1:9–13)

Baptism—Jesus Enters the Ministry (vv. 9–11)

Jesus presented Himself for John's baptism even though Jesus was sinless and needed no baptism to picture His repentance. Then why was He baptized? Jesus counted Himself a man, and made it a point to do everything God expected a man to do. Moreover, Jesus identified Himself with the sinful people He had come to save.

Jesus was baptized by John in the Jordan River. The Spirit of God descended as Jesus came up out of the water. John the Baptist saw the Spirit's descent (John 1:32), and the voice of God the Father was audible (Mark 1:11). Spirit, Son, and Father—all three persons of the Trinity were present.

Temptation—Jesus Overcomes the Adversary (vv. 12–13)

After the awesome and unique experience of His baptism, the Holy Spirit sent Jesus into the wilderness to be exposed to temptations that would test His purposes and methods. Verse 13 tells us that Jesus and Satan battled in the deepest wilderness.

Satan tempted Jesus to make Him fall, and he tempts Christians today for the same reason. As in the case of Jesus, God allows temptation to strengthen believers, not make them fall. The same Holy Spirit who gave Jesus the power to win will give believers power to win over temptation today. Although temptation is a lifetime battle, each victory prepares us to do something positive for God.

In that day, a wilderness was generally regarded as the home of evil powers and a stronghold of the devil. The temptation probably took place in the Judean wilderness.

PREACHING IN GALILEE (1:14–15)

After John the Baptist's arrest, Jesus began His Galilean ministry, preaching the good news that came from God. The world has waited and hungered for the words of verse 15:

"The time has come. The kingdom of God is near. Repent and believe the good news!"

The phrase "kingdom of God" refers to the kingly rule of God. At that time the rule of God is to be internal rather than external, over the hearts of people rather than over the military powers of the day. In a unique way, the kingdom is both present (Luke 7:18–23; 10:23–24) and yet to come (Mark 14:25; Luke 11:2).

The news demanded a response of repentance and belief in the gospel (Mark 1:15). "Believe" is the word of response that answers the question of how to receive the Good News—how to enter the kingdom. Belief is more than intellectual assent. It is trust of a person's entire being to the Good News.

CALLING FOR DISCIPLESHIP (1:16–20)

There is a lapse of time between the incidents recorded in verse 15 and those recorded in verses 16–20. The context of repenting and believing is immediately succeeded by the context of leaving and following.

A disciple is one who learns from a master or teacher.

Jesus commanded two sets of brothers, Simon Peter and Andrew and James and John, to follow Him. The brothers had followed Jesus earlier (John 1:35–42), but this call was to continuous discipleship. Immediately, they left their business and followed Jesus.

JESUS' PUBLIC MINISTRY (1:21–28)

Authoritative Teaching (vv. 21–22)

On a Sabbath day, Jesus went to the synagogue and taught (v. 21). The people were dumbfounded at the teaching of Jesus. He taught with authority rather than citing a string of footnotes as the rabbis generally did.

The timeless Good News appeared when Jesus entered His public ministry. Now, as then, it demands a verdict from the listener. Answering yes to Jesus calls for a willingness to leave everything and to risk everything.

11

Technically, the Jewish Sabbath began at sunset on Friday and ended at sunset on Saturday; but Saturday was considered the Sabbath day.

Powerful Healing (vv. 23–28)

Authoritative teaching was accompanied by powerful action. A man with an unclean spirit was in the synagogue. The demon cried out through the man, "What do you want with us, Jesus of Nazareth?"

Translated literally from the Greek text of Mark, this question reads: "What do we have in common?" But in this context, the question has the sense of, "Why do you meddle with us?"

Jesus responded to the man with a simple, authoritative command: "Be quiet! Come out of him!" The evil spirit left like a storm, with a thunderous shriek and a discharge of power that floored the man (v. 26).

Most Jewish exorcists used much magic and many words when trying to cast out a demon.

The people were amazed and responded with the question, "What is this?" (v. 27). The people were familiar with rituals for casting out demons, but they had not witnessed this kind of authority. As a result of this event, Jesus' fame began to spread quickly.

HEALINGS AT PETER'S HOUSE (1:29–34)

After they left the synagogue, Jesus and His four disciples (Andrew, Peter, James, and John) went directly to Peter's house.

Peter lived in Capernaum, a city on the northwest shore of the Sea of Galilee. Jesus made His headquarters there for His ministry throughout Galilee (2:1; 3:19; 9:33; 10:10).

Peter's mother-in-law had a high fever. When Jesus was made aware of this, He healed her. She gave evidence of complete healing and showed her gratitude by ministering to Jesus and His disciples.

Mark then tells us that a steady stream of suffering humanity flooded the door of Peter's house.

They waited until sundown—the time when the Sabbath was over—when they could carry their sick friends and family members to Jesus without violating rabbinic law.

A DOUBLE PURSUIT (1:35–39)

Jesus rose early in the morning to pray. His disciples went to look for Him and remind Him that He was now in great demand. Jesus told them He had work to do not only in Capernaum but throughout the region of Galilee.

JESUS CURES THE INCURABLE (1:40–45)

People did not consider leprosy a sin, but they did think that leprosy was an act of God and that the Messiah would be able to heal leprosy (Matt. 11:5; Luke 4:27). The Mosaic Law prescribed ceremonial cleansing for anyone whose leprosy happened to go away (which was considered a miracle of God's grace). The cleansing Jesus speaks of in Mark 1:44 is detailed in Leviticus 14:1–32. The leper had confidence Jesus could heal him if He chose to. Jesus expressed His willingness and then simply commanded the leper to be clean.

Jesus sternly charged the healed leper not to tell who had healed him, then sent the man out to the priest to have his healing officially confirmed (vv. 43–44). But the healed leper couldn't keep silent about the source of his healing.

Leprosy

Leprosy is a generic term generally applied to a variety of skin disorders from psoriasis to true leprosy. Its symptoms ranged from white patches on the skin to running sores to the loss of fingers and toes. It was terminal, but it seemed interminable because it sometimes lasted for as long as thirty years. Its suffering went beyond the physical, for its victims also suffered psychologically. Heartbreaking loneliness accompanied the leper's physical pain and mental anguish.

- *Mark's Gospel's is fast-paced and action-ori-*
- *ented. It opens with Jesus' baptism, tempta-*
- *tion, the call of the four disciples, and the*
- *early ministry in Galilee. The kingdom of*
- *God, a major theme of the Gospel, is much in*
- *evidence as Jesus delivered people from dis-*
- *eases, including leprosy, and demons.*

QUESTIONS TO GUIDE YOUR STUDY

1. What was John the Baptist's role? What was the content of his message?
2. What is significant about Jesus' baptism? Why did He insist on receiving it?
3. Why was it so important for Jesus to experience the temptation in the wilderness?
4. From the account of the many people who sought Jesus' healing help, what do we learn about the character of Jesus?

MARK 2

WHICH IS EASIER? (2:1–12)

Jesus was back in Capernaum, apparently teaching at Peter's house. Four men brought a friend who was paralyzed for Jesus to heal. They couldn't get in the house because of the crowd. So they took their friend up on the roof, made a hole in the roof, and lowered their friend down in the presence of Jesus.

Jesus had compassion on the man and told him that his sins were forgiven. This statement brought a strongly negative response in the minds of the scribes who were looking on. They didn't say anything, but Jesus knew what they were thinking.

The scribes were the grammatical and editorial nitpickers of their day. Although they were laymen with another occupation to make their living, it was their job to copy the biblical texts, keep them pure, and expound their meaning. We owe a lot to good grammarians and editors, but it is easy to see how these first-century scribes would find it hard to accept change. Later the scribes would be joined in their criticism and opposition to Jesus by Pharisees, elders, priests, Sadducees, and Herodians as well as the fickle crowds and the spineless Roman rulers.

Jesus asked them whether it was easier to tell a person his sins were forgiven or to command a paralyzed person to stand up and walk. Jesus then commanded the man to walk. He did, and the crowd was amazed.

The Typical House in Jesus' Day

The homes of the poor were small and modest, generally consisting of one to four rooms, and almost always including a courtyard on the east of the house so the prevailing westerly winds would blow the smoke away from the house. The only escape from the dim, cramped interior of the house was the courtyard and especially the flat roof.

The roof was supported by beams laid across the tops of narrow rooms, which were then covered by brush and packed with mud to a firm and smooth surface. The paralytic at Capernaum was let down to Jesus through a hole "dug out" of such a roof (Mark 2:4). It was covered with clay tiles (Luke 5:19).

Capernaum was a customs center where Levi worked. He was an unlikely prospect for discipleship because he bore the stigma of having sold out to Rome. His job was to collect taxes for a foreign people who occupied the country, and he also lived off of those taxes.

SUDDEN SURRENDER (2:13–17)

Jesus next called a tax collector named Levi (commonly known as Matthew) as a disciple. Levi not only responded positively to Jesus' call; he gave a party and invited his friends to meet Jesus. The religious leaders criticized Jesus for keeping company with these men. Jesus said He had not come to call good people but sinners.

FASTING (2:18–22)

Jesus' critics found two practices that were out of step with their traditions: fasting and observance of the Sabbath.

Those who followed John the Baptist and those who followed the way of the Pharisees may have fasted for different reasons, but fasting was a part of the religious observance of both groups. However, the Old Testament commanded fasting only once a year: on the Day of Atonement (Exod. 20:10; Lev. 16:1–4; 23:26–32; 25:9; Num. 29:9–11). By the New Testament era, Pharisees were fasting regularly on Mondays and Thursdays and seemingly making quite a show of it. Fasting could accompany repentance, or it could serve as a sign of mourning. Except for the Day of Atonement, though, fasting was a matter of choice that had become a tradition.

Jesus answered the question about fasting by saying that fasting is a practice done in connection with funerals and grieving but is completely out of place at a wedding. Jesus pictured Himself as the bridegroom and His disciples as the wedding guests. The principle He set forth is that circumstances should dictate the time of fasting.

Verses 21–22 contain two brief parables.

Parable one: The unshrunk cloth. The unshrunk cloth of the new covenant cannot be patched onto the worn-out garment of Judaism (v. 21).

Tradition has its place, but it also has its time. When the time is up, it is right to change and move forward under God's guidance.

Parable two: Old and new wineskins. Likewise, the covenant wine cannot be kept in the rigid, old wineskin of Judaism. Fresh wine should be put in unused wineskins, which are flexible enough to expand without bursting.

The point of these two parables is that Jesus knew His message called for dramatic change, and that only those who were flexible enough to receive new truth could make the transition.

PRECEDENT AND PRIORITY (2:23–28)

Time and again the religious leaders accused Jesus of breaking the Sabbath. It was the Pharisees who had gotten things reversed; they had forgotten that the Sabbath is made for man and not man for the Sabbath (v. 27).

In this particular case, Jesus did not deny the charge of the Pharisees, but He defended the behavior of His disciples with a precedent from the life of David (see Mark 2:25–26; 1 Sam. 21:1–6). The Pharisees faced a dilemma: if they condemned the disciples, they would also have to condemn David. David had also broken the ceremonial law when it became necessary. So the precedent introduces the principle of verse 27: man's emergency needs have priority over the Sabbath law of complete rest.

Jesus actually restored the Sabbath to its original place of serving people rather than enslaving them.

Jesus' Self-Revelation in Mark 2

STATEMENT OF SELF-REVELATION	VERSE
"The Son of Man has authority on earth to forgive sins"	v. 10
"The bridegroom" of the church	vv. 19–20
"The Son of Man is Lord even of the Sabbath."	v. 28

"Son of Man"

Jesus' statements of self-revelation point to aspects of His earthly ministry, such as His authority to forgive sins and to interpret the meaning of the Sabbath. Three categories of "Son of Man" sayings in the Gospels are generally recognized: those that present Him in His earthly role, those that highlight His suffering, and those that point to His glory. In general, the title "Son of Man" focuses more on Christ's divinity than His humanity. It should be viewed as pointing to Jesus' special role. He is the one who has authority to forgive sins (Matt. 9:6; Mark 2:10; Luke 5:24).

■ *Jesus' exercise of authority and His friendship*
■ *with sinners quickly got the attention of the*
■ *religious leaders, leading to their opposition.*

QUESTIONS TO GUIDE YOUR STUDY

1. The paralytic's friends sought Jesus to heal the man's physical problem. What did Jesus do?
2. This chapter introduces the element of conflict in response to Jesus' ministry. What kinds of conflicts did He encounter?
3. Mark records two parables in this chapter: the parable of the unshrunk cloth and the parable of the old and new wineskins. What point do these parables make?
4. Through His ministry, Jesus reveals who He is. What statements of self-revelation do we see in this chapter?

In this chapter the theme of controversy is again prominent. The religious leaders clashed with Jesus about their ideas of what may be done on the Sabbath and over the source of Jesus' power to exorcise evil spirits. Other major themes include the choosing of twelve disciples (vv. 13–19) and the sin of blasphemy of the Holy Spirit (vv. 28–30).

RELIGIOUS RIGOR MORTIS (3:1–6)

Jesus entered a synagogue and encountered a man with a shriveled hand. Jesus restored this man's hand. A number of Pharisees watched intently. These Pharisees went from this occasion to conspire with the Herodians to put Jesus to death.

The Herodians

The Herodians catered to the Romans. They are mentioned in only three places in the New Testament (Matt. 22:16; Mark 3:6; 12:13).

The sick people literally threw themselves against Jesus in their belief that mere contact would bring a cure (v. 10). Jesus did not mind touching or being touched by the untouchables (Mark 1:40–41); but the crowd was about to crush Him. So Jesus told His disciples to keep a boat ready in case He needed to move out into the water.

- *Jesus felt both anger and grief at the reaction*
- *of the Pharisees to His healing a man on the*
- *Sabbath.*

MINISTERING AND BEING MISUNDERSTOOD (3:7–35)

Jesus continued His Galilean ministry, which now enters a new phase. It changes location, attracts a more varied congregation, and includes the calling of twelve special disciples.

A Seaside Retreat (vv. 7–12)
Jesus and His disciples retreated to the seaside. Wherever Jesus went, He was pursued by the crowds, not only from Galilee but in the regions northwest, south, and east of Galilee.

A Mountaintop Experience (vv. 13–19a)
From the seaside, Jesus hiked to a mountaintop experience. From the multitude He selected a choice group to gather before Him on the hillside (v. 13). And from that group Jesus formally appointed the Twelve who would serve as His disciples and apostles.

The Twelve Apostles

NAME	MEANING OF NAME
Simon	"hearing" (Hebrew)
Andrew	"manliness" (Greek)
James	"Jacob" (Hebrew)
John	"the Lord is gracious" (Hebrew)
Philip	"horse lover" (Greek)
Bartholomew	"son of Talmai" (Hebrew)
Thomas	"twin" (Hebrew)
Matthew	"God has given" (Hebrew)
James "the younger"	"Jacob" (Hebrew); "the small one"
Thaddaeus	from "breast" and "heart" (Hebrew)

The Twelve Apostles

NAME	MEANING OF NAME
Simon the Zealot	"zealous one" (Greek)
Judas Iscariot	"man of Kerioth" (Hebrew)

■ *From the multitude of followers, Jesus*
■ *selected a choice group of twelve disciples.*

Mistaken Concern about Jesus (vv. 19b–27)

Jesus returned home to eat and rest (perhaps in Simon Peter's home). While speaking to the teachers of the law who came down from Jerusalem, Jesus' family arrived to "rescue" Him, for they believed He was "out of his mind." From their point of view, Jesus was taking imprudent risks and was not getting the food and rest He needed.

One of the prevailing beliefs of that culture was that stronger demons had power over weaker demons.

The teachers of the law, with whom Jesus was talking, explained Jesus' effectiveness in casting out demons by saying that He did so through the power of Beelzebub—the prince of demons.

Jesus answered the scribes' charge by questioning whether Satan would cast out Satan: "How can Satan drive out Satan?" (v. 23). His point was that a kingdom that is divided against itself cannot stand.

A Permanent Sin (vv. 28–30)

At this point, Jesus gave one of the gravest warnings ever given to human beings. Blasphemy against the Holy Spirit is a unique sin. It is the only sin for which there is no forgiveness.

Many commentators have wisely suggested that fear of having committed the unpardonable sin is the best assurance a person can have that he is not yet guilty. Coming to know the saving grace of God through Jesus Christ is the only way to be assured of never committing the unpardonable sin.

People who blaspheme the Holy Spirit reveal a spiritual condition that is incapable of the one condition of forgiveness: that is, repentance. Many biblical scholars say blasphemy of the Holy Spirit is an enduring condition, not a temporary act of sin. In a manner of speaking, when the optic nerve of the soul becomes severed, a person lacks moral discernment; and he may judge that holy acts come from an unholy spirit rather than from the Holy Spirit of God.

Proof of Spiritual Kinship (vv. 31–35)

Jesus' family arrived. They wanted to take Jesus home with them. But Jesus told them that commitment to God must have priority—even over family.

Jesus knew from Scripture that commitment to God must have priority when choosing between God and family (Exod. 32:25–29; Deut. 33:8–9).

■ *From the multitude of followers, Jesus*
■ *selected a choice group of twelve disciples.*
■ *Opposition to Jesus grew stronger. His ene-*
■ *mies said that Beelzebub was behind His*
■ *mighty acts of casting out demons.*

QUESTIONS TO GUIDE YOUR STUDY

1. What was the issue behind Jesus' healing of the man with the shriveled hand? What lesson did Jesus teach from this encounter?

2. What is the difference between an *apostle* and a *disciple*? What does a disciple do?

3. What is the sin of blasphemy against the Holy Spirit? Why is it unforgivable?

4. Why did Jesus refuse to listen to the pleas of His family and friends and go on preaching?

JESUS TEACHES IN PARABLES (4:1–32)

Mark 4 gives an account of Jesus' teaching in parables. In this setting, Jesus taught from a boat anchored just off shore. The crowd was on the shore. The water provided the amplification needed to communicate with the crowd.

The Kingdom Parables of Mark 4

PARABLE	THEME	MAIN TRUTH
Parable of the Sower	Response of God's Word	Only "good-soil" hearers will receive the Word and bear fruit.
Parable of the Lamp	Responsibility of those in the kingdom	Each Christian is like a lamp, lighted for the one purpose of illuminating the Good News.
Parable of the Seed Growing	Certainty of growth in the kingdom	The kingdom's growth is certain when the seed and the right soil get together, for God assures its growth.
Parable of the Mustard Seed	Completion of the kingdom	When time ends, and the kingdom is complete, God's rule and authority will be complete.

The Purpose of Parables

Parables were simple stories from everyday life that shed light on profound spiritual truths. Parables helped make abstract teachings concrete and meaningful—moving from the known to the unknown. Parables left men and women wondering and thinking for themselves rather than dismissing and forgetting truths that were beyond their understanding.

The trip from Capernaum on the northwestern shore to the eastern shore of the Sea of Galilee is about six miles.

PARABLE EPILOGUE (4:33–34)

Jesus spoke to the crowds in parables. He gave more extensive explanations of His teachings to His disciples.

JESUS' POWER OVER NATURE (4:35–41)

As the disciples got halfway across the Sea of Galilee on their way to Gadara, they got caught in the middle of a dangerous storm. Fearing for their lives, they awoke Jesus, who was sleeping through the ordeal. He calmed the disciples and commanded the winds and seas to "Quiet! Be still!" The storm immediately disappeared. In the calming of the wind and sea, God in Christ overruled the disorder of nature.

- *Jesus taught in parables. The theme of His*
- *teaching was the kingdom of God. Jesus dem-*
- *onstrated His lordship over nature when He*
- *calmed a storm on the Sea of Galilee.*

QUESTIONS TO GUIDE YOUR STUDY

1. What is the "kingdom of God"?
2. Why did Jesus choose to teach by using parables?
3. Mark records four parables of Jesus in this chapter. What is the main point of each? What do we learn collectively from these truths?
4. What is the lesson of Jesus' calming of the storm? How might that lesson apply to believers today?

Jesus' Displays of Power in Chapter 5

MIRACLE	PASSAGE	SIGNIFICANCE
Jesus heals the demoniac	vv. 1–20	Jesus' power over demons
Jesus heals the woman with a disease	vv. 21–34	Jesus' power over disease
Jesus raises Jarius's daughter from the dead	vv. 35–43	Jesus' power over death

Today some would say that this man whom Jesus healed was demon-possessed, while others would say he was mentally ill. The Bible often speaks of demons as literal beings and offers no apology or detailed explanation.

JESUS' POWER OVER DEMONS (5:1–20)

Upon arriving at Gadara, Jesus met a demon-possessed man. Knowing that Jesus would expel them from the man, the demons begged Jesus to let them go into the two thousand hogs nearby. Jesus granted them their request, and the evil spirits left the man and entered the pigs. The herd rushed down the steep bank into the lake and were drowned.

The man, now whole, wanted to come with Jesus. But Jesus told him to go back home and tell people what God had done for him.

JESUS' POWER OVER DISEASE (5:21–34)

Once again Jesus crossed the sea and met a crowd. This time the crowd included a synagogue ruler (or administrator) named Jairus. Jairus's little daughter lay near death. So he forgot both his personal pride and the dignity of his office as he fell at Jesus' feet and begged Jesus to come and heal his daughter. Jairus's request was urgent, and Jesus' response was immediate: He started to Jairus's home, and the crowd followed (vv. 21–24).

Her condition was desperate. She was poor, weak, ceremonially unclean (Lev. 15:25–27). Undoubtedly, the woman had tried all of the eleven cures prescribed in the Talmud (a book of Jewish writings).

On the way to Jairus's home, a woman who had suffered with a disease for twelve years silently pushed through the crowd, hoping to steal a miracle from Jesus.

She touched the hem of Jesus' garment with the faith that she would be healed. Instantly, after twelve years of misery, she was healed.

JESUS' POWER OVER DEATH (5:35–43)

In the meantime, Jairus's daughter had died and his messengers saw no need for Jairus to bother Jesus any more. Jesus told Jairus to stop being afraid and to keep on believing. Jesus went to Jairus's house and told the girl to "get up!" Immediately the girl stood up and walked around.

- ■ *Jesus showed His power over demons, incur-*
- ■ *able disease, and even death. He replaced*
- ■ *fear with faith.*

QUESTIONS TO GUIDE YOUR STUDY

1. What is Mark's focus in this chapter?
2. Why do you believe Jesus allowed the demons to inhabit the two thousand hogs, only to have them drown in the lake?
3. What was the response of the healed demonic?
4. What lessons might we, as modern believers, learn from the events of this chapter?

MARK 6

In this chapter Mark provides accounts of some of the best-known events in the Gospels: the sending out of the Twelve; the beheading of John the Baptist; Jesus' feeding of the five thousand; and Jesus walking on the water.

NO POWER OVER UNBELIEF (6:1–6)

Jesus and His disciples returned to Nazareth of Galilee, where the people refused to accept Jesus for who He was—the Messiah. Their unbelief was a barrier to the exercise of Jesus' power, so He did no powerful work there.

TRAINED FOR SERVICE (6:7–13)

Jesus called the disciples to be with Him for training so they could go out and serve Him. Jesus divided the Twelve into twos and gave them power for the work that lay ahead. The disciples had the authority of the One who sent them. They healed the sick, drove out demons, and called their hearers to repent.

A COMMISSION FULFILLED (6:14–29)

Herod feared that Jesus was a resurrected John the Baptist. At this point Mark chooses to flashback to give an account of John the Baptist's unjust arrest and murder by Herod.

JESUS FEEDS FIVE THOUSAND (6:30–56)

The apostles returned from their mission. Because of the disciples' fatigue and the pressing crowds, Jesus suggested a spiritual retreat. So they set sail for a quiet, restful place across the lake.

The only rest Jesus and the disciples got, however, was on the boat during the crossing. When Jesus and His disciples got off the boat, they

All the people touched by Jesus' power in Mark 4:35–6:6 accent the nature of His power: power over nature, power over demons, power over disease, power over death. But this picture ends in discord, for there was no power He could exercise over unbelief.

Jewish custom and Scripture required that there be two witnesses to attest a truth (Num. 35:30; Deut. 17:6).

were met by the fleet-footed crowd who had beaten them to their place of retreat.

It is about a four-mile voyage across the lake (where Jesus and the disciples crossed) and about ten miles around the lake on foot.

Jesus taught the crowds until the afternoon grew late, and then startled the disciples by saying, "You give them something to eat." The disciples objected because of the cost of such an undertaking. The disciples had forgotten that Jesus could use and multiply whatever they had for whatever need existed. They found five barley loaves and two fish. Jesus blessed the food, broke it, and gave it to His disciples for distribution. Miraculously, there was enough food for everyone, with twelve baskets of food left over.

This miracle of the feeding of the five thousand is the only miracle found in all four Gospels.

Following the miracle of the feeding of the five thousand, Jesus quickly ordered the disciples to sail while He dismissed the crowd. After retreating to a hillside to pray, Jesus saw that the disciples' boat was caught in a storm on the sea. Jesus walked on the water to their boat, and got in the boat with them. The sea immediately calmed down. The experience left the disciples dumbfounded.

John's Gospel explains this quick dismissal of the crowd. They were about to make Him king. The crowd's expectations of Jesus ran counter to God's will for Him.

As Jesus' boat drew near the western shore of the Sea of Galilee, the crowds immediately recognized Him. He ministered to many who needed healing. His tireless, selfless service is a lesson for His followers.

■ *Jesus continued to show His lordship over*
■ *every dimension of life. He empowered His*
■ *disciples for multiplying His work in the*
■ *towns and villages of Galilee.*

QUESTIONS TO GUIDE YOUR STUDY

1. What was the response of Jesus' hometown and His relatives? Why did the people view Him as they did?

2. Describe the sending out of the Twelve. What was Jesus' goal with this mission?

3. What lesson did the disciples learn from the feeding of the five thousand?

4. What did the disciples learn (and what can we learn) from Jesus' rescue of the disciples in the storm?

A MAN-MADE RELIGION (7:1–8)

The Pharisees and scribes condemned Jesus and His disciples for breaking "the tradition of the elders" because they had failed to observe ritual handwashing before they ate. In their efforts to be separate, the religious leaders failed to understand that the condition of a person's heart toward God and man is the basis for God to judge a person as being holy.

The title Pharisees means "separated ones."

A RELIGIOUS TRAVESTY (7:9–23)

Jesus continued His attack against man-made rules that contradict the command of God. Exodus 20:12 and 21:17 clearly show that a person is responsible for his parents (Mark 7:10). Yet, the religious lawyers had invented a mythical loophole for commandment evasion. Jesus answered the religious leaders by condemning their hypocrisy.

Corban was a Hebrew word that was used in the last centuries B.C. and the first century A.D. in a dedication formula. The word was used in the Old Testament to indicate a gift to God. During Jesus' earthly ministry, Corban was used by the Pharisees and scribes and their followers to indicate the setting aside of something as a gift to God or as a Temple gift.

Jesus explained to the crowd, and later in greater detail to His disciples, that it was not a man's eating habits that made him "unclean." The body's natural process is to take anything that enters the stomach and pass it out of the body. But a person's spiritual condition is revealed by that which is "within" the heart. If the heart is unclean, then evil words and deeds will be the result.

FAITH THAT BRINGS A RESPONSE (7:24–37)

For all practical purposes, Jesus' Galilean ministry is over, and He traveled to the region of Tyre and Sidon. This withdrawal begins an extensive circular journey that is Jesus' longest recorded trip.

A Mother's Faith (vv. 24–30)

A woman whose daughter was possessed by an unclean spirit or demon believed that Jesus had the power to heal her daughter. Jesus tested the mother's faith and she persisted in recognizing Jesus as Lord. Jesus pronounced the daughter healed because of the woman's expression of faith. What made the woman's faith unique was that she would not take no for an answer. Her faith was real.

Faithful Friends (vv. 31–37)

Friends of a man who was deaf and had a speech impediment wanted Jesus to lay His hands on the man for blessing or healing. Jesus took the man aside and privately pantomimed with divine sign language the healing that would take place. After Jesus touched the man's ears and placed the saliva on his tongue, Jesus prayed, "Be opened!" Instantly, the man heard and spoke clearly.

Those familiar with the Old Testament saw the miracle as a reminder of Isaiah 35:4–6, which gives a preview of the Messiah's healing actions.

- *Jesus exposed the hypocrisy of religion that is*
- *so focused on externals that it loses touch*
- *with matters that most concern God.*

QUESTIONS TO GUIDE YOUR STUDY

1. Why did the religious leaders condemn the disciples? What was Jesus' response to the leaders?

2. What was the religious leaders' "tradition of the elders"? What did Jesus have to say to them? What lesson did He give to the crowd that had gathered?

3. Jesus healed a woman's daughter who was possessed by an unclean spirit or demon. Jesus rewarded her faith. What

lessons might we learn from this woman about the nature of genuine faith?

4. In verses 31–35, Jesus healed a man who could not hear or speak. How did Jesus heal the man?

FAITH AT WORK (8:1–10)

Mark's next account pictures four thousand hungry people in the desert with no food to eat. Because Jesus' followers had been with Him for three days, they had run out of provisions. As He had fed the five thousand earlier (6:30–44), Jesus now also feeds the four thousand.

Jesus can do great things with small resources.

A FAITHLESS REQUEST (8:11–13)

Some Pharisees challenged Jesus to give them a sign to prove His messiahship or authority. It is obvious that their motive was not a desire to believe in Jesus but a desire to discredit Him. His life and ministry are enough for those who really want to believe. The only sign He will give will be the sign of Jonah (Matt. 12:39–40).

The Old Testament prophet Jonah was in the stomach of the fish three days and nights. Jesus will die, be buried, and rise from death on the third day.

BEWARE OF THE YEAST (8:14–21)

The disciples became concerned when they discovered they had only one loaf of bread with them in the boat. Jesus cautioned His disciples to guard against the yeast of the Pharisees and the yeast of Herod.

Yeast was leaven. It symbolized moral influence—whether good or bad. However, more often than not, it stood for bad (Matt. 16:6; Luke 12:1), and it stands for evil in verse 15.

Jesus did not want the evil thinking of the Pharisees to contaminate their faith. They had witnessed Jesus' miraculous feeding of five thousand people and then four thousand people. Being in Jesus' presence, how could they be concerned about having just one loaf of bread?

A RESPONSE TO FAITH (8:22–26)

After so many examples of spiritual blindness, Jesus healed a man who was physically blind. This miracle was done in private and saliva was used, but it is unique in that the healing came gradually in two stages instead of happening instantly.

TURNING POINT (8:27)

Mark 8:27 divides the book of Mark. Up to this point in the book, the emphasis has been upon Jesus' ministry. From Mark 8:27 onward, the emphasis is on Jesus' approaching suffering, death, and resurrection.

THE DISCIPLES' UNDERSTANDING TESTED (8:27–33)

From Bethsaida, Jesus and His disciples went north about twenty-five miles to the villages around Caesarea Philippi. The city itself was named after Caesar, and it was an area where Caesar was looked upon as lord.

The title *Christ* was Greek, and *Messiah* was Hebrew for "the Anointed One."

In this passage Jesus questioned the disciples about His identity by asking them who other people said He was. Jesus then asked the disciples, "Who do you say I am?" Like a rifle shot, Peter answered, "You are the Christ." Because Jesus was not ready to reveal His messiahship, He commanded their silence concerning this matter.

The prevailing Jewish idea of how the Messiah would establish His kingdom included military violence that would be destructive and a nationalistic spirit that would be vengeful (cp. 2 Sam. 7:14–16 and Jer. 23:5–6 with Isa. 53:3–5).

Jesus reeducated the disciples about the meaning of discipleship. Jesus referred to Himself as "the Son of man" who must suffer, be rejected, die, and rise again. Messiah is a suffering servant. The disciples' gladness turned to sadness when Jesus began to reveal more fully what it meant to be Messiah.

THE COST OF DISCIPLESHIP (8:34–9:1)

After telling what price He would pay for man's redemption, Jesus revealed what it would cost a person who really *wanted* to follow Him. Verse 34 sets forth three conditions of discipleship: denying oneself; taking up a daily cross; and continual loyalty to Jesus.

Mark's early readers were enduring persecution, and the words of Jesus must have been an encouraging challenge to continue the Christian life in the face of death.

Most scholars believe that "the kingdom of God come with power" (9:1) refers to one or more of the following:

1. the transfiguration
2. the resurrection of Jesus
3. the gift of the Spirit at Pentecost
4. the expansion of the early church.
(See Matt. 16:27–28 and Rom. 1:4 for related texts.)

- *Jesus took His disciples on a retreat. In that*
- *setting, Peter confessed Jesus was the Mes-*
- *siah. Jesus began to explain the implications*
- *of His being Messiah—both for Him and for*
- *His disciples.*

QUESTIONS TO GUIDE YOUR STUDY

1. As Jesus had fed the five thousand (6:30–44), He now also fed the four thousand. What truths about Jesus does this story teach us?

2. Why did Jesus rebuke the disciples in verses 17–21? What did He specifically say to them?

3. What were the marks of Jesus' messiahship? Why did the disciples have a difficult time accepting these?

4. What is the cost of discipleship, as revealed by Jesus Himself?

THE TRANSFIGURATION (9:2–8)

This event occurred most likely on Mount Hermon (elevation 9,100 ft.). Its name means "devoted mountain" and stands at the northern boundary of Israel.

As a preparation for the difficult road ahead, Jesus took Peter, James, and John up on a high mountain. There for a brief time, God allowed them to see the glory of Jesus. He was transfigured before their eyes. Moses and Elijah appeared and talked with Jesus. Moses represents the Law and Elijah the Prophets. Jesus is the fulfillment of all that is written in the Law and the Prophets.

GOD'S PLAN OF REDEMPTION (9:9–13)

"Transfiguration"

Every Christian has the promise of a future transfiguration. Interestingly, the Greek word for transfigured or transformed (used in v. 2) is applied in Romans 12:1–2 and 2 Corinthians 3:18 to obedient Christians who let God transform their lives.

With Elijah's image fresh in their minds, the disciples wanted Jesus to explain the teachings about Elijah's return before the coming of the Messiah. Jesus explained that John had fulfilled the role of Elijah in the sense that he had turned people back to God in repentance and forgiveness.

FAITH'S QUALITY (9:14–29)

After descending from the mountain, Jesus was greeted by powerless disciples, arguing scribes, and a brokenhearted father with an epileptic son. The debate was focused on the epileptic boy. The disciples had failed to cast out from the boy the evil spirit endangering his life.

The father asked Jesus to help the boy if He could. "If I can?" Jesus replied, assuring the father that all things are possible to those who believe.

The father cried out to the Lord, "I do believe; help me overcome my unbelief!"

Jesus healed the boy.

Privately, the disciples asked why they hadn't been able to cast out the demon. Jesus explained that this kind of demon could be driven out only by prayers of faith (vv. 19, 29). (The best Greek manuscripts do not include fasting as a requirement for casting out demons.)

A PROPHETIC PROMISE (9:30–32)

Jesus wanted to be alone with His disciples to teach them further about His messiahship. He tried to impress upon them the price and promise of redemption. They found it difficult to grasp Jesus' kingship and His certainty of resurrection.

MISPLACED COMMITMENT (9:33–37)

On the way to Capernaum, Jesus taught His disciples about greatness. They were confusing greatness with grandness and were still committed to selfish goals. Jesus explained that if they wanted to be first and great, they had to be last and least.

MOTIVE, NOT METHOD, IS WHAT COUNTS (9:38–41)

John and the other disciples did not want anyone to use Jesus' name authoritatively to cast out demons unless he was a part of Jesus' company. Jesus told the disciples to test a person's commitment by his motive, not his method.

TOTAL COMMITMENT (9:42–50)

Jesus warned His disciples that it would be tragic for anyone to trip up any of His children who tried to follow Him. Causing others to stumble into sin is a serious offense. He emphasized that the cost of discipleship is great, teaching that believers are to have purity, zeal, and fellowship.

Both The New International Version and the New Revised Standard Version omit verses 44 and 46, as do the most ancient manuscripts. But those verses are identical with verse 48, which depicts the awfulness of hell.

- *Three of the disciples witnessed the transfig-*
- *uration of Jesus. In spite of this experience,*
- *some of these same disciples argued over who*
- *was the greatest—showing that they had not*
- *yet understood what Jesus' kingdom was all*
- *about.*

QUESTIONS TO GUIDE YOUR STUDY

1. Describe Mark's account of the transfiguration. What was its significance?
2. What lesson did Jesus teach with the healing of the demon-possessed boy?
3. Why were the disciples arguing about greatness? What lesson did Jesus teach them about true greatness?
4. What do we learn from verses 42–50 about the commitment to discipleship?

Mark 8:27–9:50 focuses on Jesus' teaching about His messiahship and what it means to follow the Messiah. In Mark 10 Jesus seems to turn on one light after another until He has illuminated the full meaning of discipleship.

Mark 9 formally ends Jesus' Galilean ministry. Mark 10–15 records the Judean ministry. However, from the turning point of Mark 8:27 onward, there is a sense in which only the name *Jerusalem* is really important. Everything will eventually come to a climax in Jerusalem.

Jesus' Ministry in Mark

Region of Ministry	Passage in Mark
Galilee (Early)	1:14–3:6
Galilee (Later)	3:7–6:13
Judea	10:1–15
Ideals—Not Ideas	10:1–12

THE PHARISEES' UNDERSTANDING OF DIVORCE (10:1–4)

Once again Jesus was surrounded by crowds. As usual, He taught them. The "all-knowing" Pharisees who came to Jesus were just the opposite of learners. They had come not to receive knowledge from Jesus, but to trap Him with a question. They asked Him: "Is it lawful for a man to divorce his wife?" (Mark 10:2).

Of course, any answer Jesus gave would put Him in conflict with one of the pharisaic ideas about divorce (see Matt. 19:1–9). As the parallel

Rabbinic Teachings on Divorce

Deuteronomy 24:1 was generally accepted as a statement of legal procedure for divorce, but there were two rabbinic schools that held opposite and extreme views on reasons for divorce. The school of Hillel believed that a man could divorce his wife for almost any reason: spoiling the food, dancing in the streets, talking with a strange man, letting her husband hear her speak disrespectfully about her in-laws, being a loud-mouthed, brawling woman. One rabbi even extended the reason for divorce as being adequate if the husband should find someone he liked better than his wife. In contrast, the school of Shammai gave adultery as the only reason for divorce.

account in Matthew reveals (19:3–12), the basic question is not whether divorce was permitted but for what reasons it might be permitted.

JESUS' CLARIFICATION OF THE TEACHING ON DIVORCE (10:5–12)

The Pharisees tried to trap Jesus with the question: "Is it lawful for a man to divorce his wife?" Jesus changed the question and turned it back on the Pharisees, asking them what Moses had commanded. Jesus showed the Pharisees that God intended for a man and woman to marry, leave their parents, become one, and discipline themselves to live together for life.

THE ESSENTIAL QUALITIES OF DISCIPLESHIP (10:13–16)

Using children as an object lesson, Jesus taught about kingdom citizenship. Disciples are to portray the same traits as these children—trust, humility, and obedience.

ONE WAY TO DISCIPLESHIP (10:17–22)

A rich young ruler came to Jesus and asked what he could do to inherit eternal life, thinking that he could perform some act to inherit it. Jesus gave him the formula for discipleship: go, sell, give, come, and follow me. Because the ruler could not surrender his possessions, he went away in despair.

THE ABSOLUTE GRACE OF GOD (10:23–27)

Jesus commented to His disciples that it is hard for the wealthy to enter the kingdom of God. It is easier for a camel to go through the eye of a needle than for a rich man to enter the kingdom of God. The disciples were amazed, for Jewish people equated wealth with the special favor of God.

Divorce and the Law in Jesus' Day

According to Jewish law, a man could not be charged with adultery against his own wife, but she could be charged with adultery against her husband (Deut. 22:13–30). (However, the husband could he charged with adultery against another man's wife.) Under Roman law, a woman could divorce her husband, but under Jewish law a woman could not divorce her husband, technically speaking. Under Jewish law the act of divorce remained as the husband's act, but the wife could claim various reasons as justification for divorce. Some examples were: denial of sexual rights, impotence, leprosy, entrance into a disgusting trade, and other select reasons. Under Jewish law the woman was discriminated against.

THE DIVIDENDS OF DISCIPLESHIP (10:28–31)

Peter told Jesus that he and the other disciples had left all to follow Jesus. His implication was that they had done what Jesus commanded; "what are we going to get in return?" Jesus answered Peter with three prophetic promises: (1) one hundred times as much as a disciple gives up for the sake of Christ and the gospel; (2) the challenge of persecutions; and (3) the fulfillment of eternal life, which has already begun for those who trust Jesus.

DISCIPLES UNTO DEATH (10:32–44)

On the way to Jerusalem, Jesus paused along the way to give His disciples a third major prophecy about His approaching death and resurrection. He announced that He would be betrayed, condemned, mocked, flogged, and killed.

We can see this increasing vividness in prophecy in chart form:

"The eye of a needle"

The word for *eye* means "hole, perforation, opening." The needle's eye was considered the smallest opening. The camel was the largest animal that came to mind. However, twice in the Talmud (Jewish writings), there is reference to the impossibility of an elephant's passing through the eye of a needle. In the picturesque language of the Hebrews, impossible comparisons were often used to make a point.

Events Prophesied About Christ	Mark 8:31	Mark 9:31	Mark 10:33–34	Suffering Narrative*
1. Betrayed/delivered to chief-priests and scribes	✓	✓	✓	14:53
2. Rejected/condemned by chief priests and scribes	✓	—	✓	14:64
3. Handed over to Romans (Gentiles)	—	—	✓	15:1
4. Humiliated and beaten	—	—	✓	14:65; 15:1–20
5. Executed	✓	✓	✓	15:24
6. Resurrected	✓	✓	✓	16:9

*(This chart is adapted from commentaries by Vincent Taylor, The Gospel According to St. Mark [London: Macmillan & Co., LTD, 1959; New York: St. Martin's Press, 1959]; and William L. Lane, The New International Commentary on the New Testament: Commentary on the Gospel of Mark [Grand Rapids: Eerdmans, 1974], as published in Johnnie C. Godwin, Mark, Layman's Bible Book Commentary [Nashville: Broadman & Holman Publishers, 1979], p. 88.)

STANDARDS FOR GREATNESS (10:35–45)

There are a lot of standards for judging greatness, but there are two standards that stand in stark contrast to each other.

Worldly Standards (vv. 35–40)

In spite of all Jesus' teachings, James and John still had worldly dreams of occupying the highest positions in Jesus' kingdom. They and their mother still misunderstood the nature of the kingdom of God (Matt. 20:20–21; but also see 27:56). "Right hand" and "left hand" were Jewish terms for being next to the king in honor. Jesus graciously told the disciples that they did not know what they were asking. In fact, if Jesus had literally fulfilled James and John's request, they would have occupied the other two crosses on Golgotha; for it was on Golgotha that Christ was lifted up, then glorified by the Father.

Heavenly Standards (vv. 41–45)

Jesus taught that the heavenly standard is that whoever wants to be great must be a servant, and whoever wants to be the greatest of all must be the slave of all.

SIGHT AND DISCIPLESHIP (10:46–52)

Jesus passed a blind man, Bartimaeus, who begged Jesus to have mercy on him. Bartimaeus needed his sight, and Jesus announced that Bartimaeus' faith had made him well.

For the first time in the book of Mark, Jesus interpreted the purpose of His life. He came to die in our place (v. 45). He came as a ransom to free those who were kidnapped by sin. This word for *ransom* is used only here and in Matthew 20:28 in the New Testament. But related words that talk about "ransom," "redeem," or "redemption" appear in a number of places (see Luke 1:68; 2:38; 24:21; Titus 2:14; Heb. 9:12; 1 Pet. 1:18). The text does not press the terminology to say who receives that ransom; nor should that be as important as the deliverance of captives by the life of Christ (see Isa. 53:10–12 for the fact of Christ's death taking the place of sinful humanity).

■ *Jesus proceeded to Jerusalem, ministering*
■ *and teaching as He went.*

QUESTIONS TO GUIDE YOUR STUDY

1. What question did the Pharisees use to try to trap Jesus? What lessons did He teach from this encounter?

2. What are the essential qualities of Jesus' disciples?

3. What is the lesson of the account of the rich young ruler?

4. The disciples would often argue about who would receive the highest positions in the kingdom. What did Jesus say about standards of greatness?

Throughout Mark's Gospel, Jesus forcefully revealed His messiahship through authoritative teachings and actions. From this point on, the events occur in and around Jerusalem. There are quiet times, but there are also times of stormy conflict. In scene after scene, Jesus emerges as the undisputed Master Teacher. However, with every clash with the Jewish leaders, Jesus comes one step closer to the cross.

THE PEOPLE ACCLAIM JESUS' AUTHORITY (11:1–11)

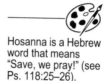

Hosanna is a Hebrew word that means "Save, we pray!" (see Ps. 118:25–26).

It was the time of Passover. The Jewish expectations for messianic deliverance were at their highest. Jesus entered Jerusalem riding a donkey, and the crowds received Him as the Messiah. They spread their outer garments and leafy branches in the road, shouting, "Hosanna! Blessed is he who comes in the name of the Lord!" Contrary to the hopes of the crowd, He was a king of peace, not a military conqueror who promised to rescue them from Roman occupation.

POWER WITH PURPOSE (11:12–14)

On His way to Jerusalem, Jesus became hungry and saw a fig tree with leaves but no fruit. With a word, Jesus caused the tree to wither. Symbolically, this mysterious event may represent Israel's unfruitfulness and approaching doom.

AUTHORITATIVE ACTION (11:15–19)

When Jesus arrived at the Temple in Jerusalem, He found that the Temple had become an unholy cattle market where worshipers were cheated out of their money. With explosive force He ended it all, driving the moneychangers out of the Temple.

Moneychangers were present at the Temple to exchange Roman or other moneys for Jewish money acceptable in the Temple worship. Worshipers could also purchase birds and animals used for sacrifice. Since sacrificial birds and animals had to be officially certified and unblemished, it was helpful to purchase them at the Temple. Some exchangers profited greatly and loaned their money. Their interest rates ranged from 20 to 300 percent per year. Evidently, the selling and money changing had become a means of cheating and exploiting the people. In anger at this corruption of the purpose of the Temple, Jesus turned over the tables of the moneychangers and drove them and the sellers of animals out of the Temple court.

Jesus' actions amazed the scribes and chief priests and struck fear in them.

ACCESS TO AUTHORITY (11:20–26)

Once again Jesus and His disciples passed the dried-up fig tree that was "withered from the roots." Jesus used this opportunity to teach His disciples the power of faith—faith that moves mountains.

A STALEMATE (11:27–33)

A religious delegation asked Jesus for His religious credentials. Jesus met the opening question with a paralyzing and defeating counter-question: Is the authority of John the Baptist from heaven or from man? To admit that John's authority was divine would be a self-condemnation for the religious leaders, and it would be an admission that Jesus was the Messiah. They were beaten. The religious leaders gave the only answer left to them: "We don't know" (v. 33).

- *Jesus entered Jerusalem riding a colt in what*
- *has come to be called the Triumphal Entry.*
- *Once in Jerusalem, He cleansed the Temple,*
- *cursed a fig tree, and was questioned by the*
- *religious leaders.*

QUESTIONS TO GUIDE YOUR STUDY

1. What is the significance of Jesus entering Jerusalem on a donkey at Passover? What were the people's expectations?
2. What is the lesson of the dried-up fig tree? What does it symbolize?
3. Jesus contrasted doubt and faith. What points did He make?
4. Jesus outmaneuvered the religious leaders who questioned His authority. How did He respond? What was their dilemma?

This chapter continues the events of the previous chapter, with Jesus following up on His discussion with the religious leaders.

THE PARABLE OF THE TENANTS (12:1–12)

Jesus followed the unanswered questions of the religious leaders with the parable of the tenants. The following chart indicates the symbolism of the parable.

The destruction of the tenants undoubtedly looked ahead to the destruction of Jerusalem that would occur in A.D. 70 when the Romans destroyed Jerusalem.

Parable of the Tenants

SYMBOL	COUNTERPART IN REALITY
The vineyard	Israel
The owner	God
The tenants	Jewish leaders
The servants	The Prophets
The son	Christ

The Pharisees thought of themselves as the purist representatives of God, who also represented the best interests of the Jewish people. The Herodians were a political party of Jews who supported Herod Antipas and, consequently, supported Rome. These two groups wanted to bait Jesus and catch Him like a fish.

Jesus concluded the parable by asking and then answering His own question about the ultimate fate of the tenants (v. 9). The religious leaders saw that the parable was directed at them. They looked for a way to arrest Jesus.

TO PAY OR NOT TO PAY? (12:13–17)

The Pharisees and Herodians, although natural enemies, united to trap Jesus. They asked Jesus if it was lawful to pay taxes to Caesar. Beyond the question of legality, they were asking whether they ought to pay or were permitted to pay the tribute. Knowing His questioners' evil motive, Jesus asked for a tax coin. By asking whose image and name were on the coin, Jesus caused His questioners to tear apart their carefully built dilemma, for they had to answer "Caesar's."

In those days people held that coinage was a sign of a king's power over his conquered land.

TWO DIFFERENT WORLDS (12:18–27)

The Sadducees now confronted Jesus. Their far-fetched and absurd example of seven brothers, one wife, and no children stemmed from what was called levirate marriage (Deut. 25:5–10; Ruth 4:5; Mark 12:19–22). (A levir was a brother-in-law.) If a brother died without any children, it was the duty of his brother to take the widow as his wife. The Sadducees used it to question Jesus and ridicule belief in the resurrection. They intended to put down Jesus as a teacher and to imply that life beyond the grave would include polygamy. Jesus informed the Sadducees that they were wrong and used Old Testament Scriptures to prove His point.

The Sadducees were priests of the Temple and came from aristocratic families of Jerusalem. The Sadducees looked to the first five books of the Bible (the Pentateuch) for their doctrinal beliefs, and they did not believe in resurrection from the dead, angels, demons, spirits, or Jesus (see Acts 23:8). The Pharisees did believe in the resurrection from the dead, angels, demons, and spirits.

AUTHORITY AND PRIORITY (12:28–34)

Jesus' response to the Sadducees impressed a scribe who wanted to know which commandment had priority over all others. Jesus told him that loving God completely is the first commandment. And, when a person gives God first love, that person will also love his or her neighbor.

SONSHIP AND LORDSHIP (12:35–37)

Jesus did not wait for questions to continue His teaching. He went to the Temple and asked questions that needed to be answered and provoked thought.

Although a descendant of David by birth, the Messiah was much more than a mere human descendant of David. His was also David's Lord by divine nature.

MISUSED AUTHORITY (12:38–40)

The scribes were seen as people of authority, for they were experts at explaining the Law of Moses. But Jesus cautioned the people against following so-called experts when they misused their authority by calling attention to it.

Jesus did not condemn all religious leaders, but He did condemn those who were guilty of hypocrisy, self-righteousness, and covetousness. Their self-centered attitudes led them to misuse authority. The need for Jesus' caution does not end with those who hear Him.

SPIRITUAL SCALES (12:41–44)

As Jesus watched the crowd put their money into the Temple treasury, He noticed a widow who gave all she had—two mites. This offering seemed meager compared to the large offerings the rich people were giving. He pointed out that from God's perspective, the greatest gift is that which costs the giver the most.

- ■ *Jesus taught in Jerusalem. His parable of the*
- ■ *tenants reinforced the intention of the reli-*
- ■ *gious leaders to arrest Him.*

QUESTIONS TO GUIDE YOUR STUDY

1. Describe the parable of the tenants. What is its main point?
2. Jesus' enemies asked Him if it was lawful to pay taxes to Caesar. What was their motive in asking this question? What was Jesus' answer?

3. What was the Sadducees' question? What was Jesus' skillful response? What was the scribe's question and Jesus' response to him?

4. What lesson can we learn from the widow who gave two mites?

The Temple in Jerusalem

Solomon's Temple was the first Temple. It was built about 960–950 B.C. The Babylonians destroyed that Temple in 581 B.C. Zerubbabel led in the building of a second Temple on the same site, and it was completed about 515 B.C. The second Temple was not bad, despite what some writers have written about it. In fact, that Temple stood for almost five hundred years, a longer time than either Solomon's Temple or Herod's Temple existed.

The Temple was on a hill that was 2,470 feet above sea level. The Temple faced the east where the sun rises over Mount Olivet, which is 200 feet higher than the Temple hill. From that vantage point, the original four disciples (Peter, James, John, and Andrew, 1:16–20) were with Jesus, who was seated in a customary teaching position.

If Mark wrote his Gospel about A.D. 65, he wrote in the middle of a chaotic decade. Christians in Rome were having to deal with Nero and his persecution. Christians in Jerusalem faced the turmoil that would come from A.D. 66–70 and would result in the destruction of Jerusalem in A.D. 70.

Mark 13 is an assurance chapter punctuated with commands on how to face the future. Its writing is prophecy and is steeped in Jewish thought and terminology about the Day of the Lord.

THE BEGINNING OF THE END FOR JERUSALEM (13:1–2)

As Jesus and His disciples left the Temple, His disciples commented on the grandeur of the Temple complex. For nearly a thousand years, the Temple site in Jerusalem had been a place of religious importance for all Jews, but it had become unholy. Jesus announced its impending destruction.

A VIEW TO THE FUTURE (13:3–8)

On the Mount of Olives, across from the Temple, the disciples wanted to know more about Jesus' prophecy of the Temple's destruction. He taught them about the specific time between the present and the destruction of Jerusalem and the general time between the present and Jesus' Second Coming.

THE DIFFICULT WAY OF DISCIPLESHIP (13:9–13)

Jesus taught the disciples about the high cost of discipleship. A characteristic of true disciples is that they endure whatever persecution comes their way, and they do not abandon their faithful following of Christ.

HOPE BEFORE THE RUINS (13:14–23)

In this section, Jesus shared the sign that will appear before Jerusalem's destruction and offer hope of escape for those who recognize the sign and leave Judea. The disciples were to be on their "guard" and watch for the signs of the impending destruction of Jerusalem.

SIGNS OF THE SAVIOR (13:24–27)

These verses refer to the Second Coming of Christ and the signs of the coming Savior. To communicate with his readers, Mark uses poetic language drawn from Old Testament background about the Day of the Lord.

The Jewish historian Josephus has given a fuller description of this destruction in his writings called the Wars.

A PARABLE OF PROMISE (13:28–31)

Jesus taught the disciples a lesson with a parable from nature. As the twigs of a fig tree get tender and the leaves come out, one knows that summer is near. Jesus told them that when they saw "these things happening," they would know that "it is near," that is, the destruction of Jerusalem.

CERTAINTIES IN UNCERTAIN TIMES (13:32–37)

No one knows when the Day of the Lord, the Second Coming of Christ, will arrive. God the Father alone knows when this event will take place.

We are to live in such a way that whether the Lord comes during the night watches or during the day, we will be ready for His return.

■ *Jesus taught regarding the near-term future*
■ *as well as events of the long-term future.*

QUESTIONS TO GUIDE YOUR STUDY

1. What is the setting for Mark 13? What three future events are associated with this chapter?

2. Why was Jerusalem to be destroyed? What was the sign of the destruction of Jerusalem? What attitude are believers to assume and what are they to do when they see the sign? Will Jerusalem's destruction be final?

3. What are characteristics of true disciples?

4. From what we read in this chapter, what are the signs of Jesus' Second Coming? What do we know about the time of His coming? What should the believer's attitude be with regard to Jesus' imminent return?

MARK 14

Mark 14 begins what is known as the "passion narrative." *Passion* basically means suffering. From this point on, Mark dealt with the events that led up to the death of Christ.

THE RELIGIOUS LEADERS PLOT TO MURDER JESUS (14:1–2)

Two days before the Passover, the chief priests were looking for the best way to end Jesus' life. The religious leaders decided to arrest Jesus privately to avoid creating a riot.

MARY ANOINTS JESUS (14:3–9)

While Jesus was eating a meal with friends at Bethany, Mary suddenly broke a vial of costly perfume and anointed Jesus' head and feet with it, and then she wiped His feet with her hair. Judas and the other disciples at first silently resented what they considered a waste of three hundred *denarii* worth of perfume (see Matt. 26:8; John 12:4–5).

Jesus' response to those who rebuked Mary was, "She poured perfume on my body beforehand to prepare for my burial."

JUDAS SELLS OUT FOR MONEY (14:10–11)

Judas betrayed Jesus, selling Him out for the price of a slave (thirty pieces of silver). He conspired with the priests and scribes to find Jesus and arrest Him.

THE DISCIPLES PREPARE FOR THE PASSOVER (14:12–16)

Jesus wanted His disciples to prepare for the Passover meal. Jesus secured a room where the disciples would be His guests for this meal.

One cannot be dogmatic about the exact chronological order of time and events of the story. The Romans kept time one way, and the Jews kept time another way. However, we do know the crucial steps of the story; and we can gain insights by studying parallel passages from the other Gospels (see Matt. 26; Luke 22; John 12:1–18:1; also see 1 Cor. 11:23–26).

A denarius was what a laboring man earned for one day's work.

Even my close friend, whom I trusted,
  he who shared my bread,
    has lifted up his heel against me.

Psalm 41:9

JESUS EXPOSES THE TRAITOR (14:17–21)

During the Passover meal, Jesus announced that one of the Twelve would betray Him. Each disciple was sad, expressing the hope that he was not the betrayer.

The Passover meal was a time to remember God's deliverance of Israel from Egypt.

BEGINNING A MEMORIAL (14:22–25)

During this Passover observance, Jesus began the memorial we know as the Lord's Supper. The broken bread symbolized Jesus' broken body. The fruit of the vine was a picture of Jesus' blood "poured out for many."

The Passover meal customarily ended with the singing of hymns of praise from the latter part of Psalms 113–118. This group of psalms is known as Hallel Psalms (or we might say Hallelujah Psalms).

Comparing Gospel Accounts

For the reader to supplement Mark's brief, quick-moving account, it is especially important to study the other Gospels for details and helpful insights. Mark 14:43–15:41 parallels the following passages from the other three Gospel accounts:

Matthew 26:47–27:56

Luke 22:47–23:49

John 18:2–19:30.

Those passages move from the betrayal of Jesus, through the trials and crucifixion, to Jesus' victorious death.

PREDICTING DESERTION AND DENIAL (14:26–31)

Jesus announced that all of the disciples would desert Him. In fact, Peter would not only desert Him, but he would also deny Him three times that night. Despite Jesus' prediction, the disciples did not consider it possible for them to desert or deny Him.

WILLING GOD'S WILL (14:32–42)

The Garden of Gethsemane, located at the foot of the Mount of Olives, became a scene of agony and victory, for here Jesus faced the alternative of avoiding death. Jesus prayed that if it were possible, He might be delivered from the cup of suffering. However, He affirmed His preference for the Father's will.

A COWARDLY ARREST (14:43–52)

Judas entered the Garden of Gethsemane and led the Sanhedrin guard to seize Jesus. Jesus voluntarily placed Himself in the custody of the mob. While Jesus remained calm, the disciples panicked and ran. Jesus foretold this (Mark 14:27), as did Zechariah (13:7). Verses 51–52 tell of a young disciple who may have been the last to run away and who nearly got caught. If this is the case, it is Mark's humble way of saying, "I was there, and I also deserted him."

A JUDICIAL FARCE (14:53–65)

Jesus had two trials with three stages each, according to the collective Gospel records: a religious trial and a civil trial. This passage focuses on the religious trial.

The Sanhedrin was made up of the high priest, former high priests (chief priests), and others who were called elders and scribes. This Jewish supreme court had access to a Temple police force that could act within certain limitations under Roman law.

A Kangaroo Court (vv. 53–54)

To try Jesus, the Sanhedrin broke its own rules. It could not meet legally until sunrise; nor could the court meet at any of the great feasts. They broke these rules and others. It is clear that the court's interest was not justice.

Lying Witnesses (vv. 55–59)

The court had trouble finding a charge that condemned Jesus to death. The false witnesses didn't give a consistent testimony.

A Blinding Truth (vv. 60–65)

Not getting anywhere with the false witnesses, the high priest asked Jesus if He was the Messiah, the Son of God. Jesus answered simply, "I am."

This response greatly angered the high priest, who tore his clothes. He charged Jesus with

According to law, at least two witnesses were needed to agree on a specific charge to make an accusation stick (Num. 35:30; Deut. 17:6; 19:15).

blasphemy—a crime punishable by death under Jewish law.

PETER: A DISCIPLE IN DENIAL (14:66–72)

In the courtyard below Jesus' trial, Peter denied his association with Jesus three times, as Jesus had predicted. Realizing what he had done, Peter wept bitterly.

- *Jesus hosted the Passover meal for His disci-*
- *ples and initiated the Lord's Supper. He was*
- *then arrested and taken first to a religious*
- *trial.*

QUESTIONS TO GUIDE YOUR STUDY

1. Why were the religious leaders determined to murder Jesus?
2. What was the cup Jesus asked the Father to deliver from Him? What did He accomplish in the Garden of Gethsemane?
3. What kind of religious trial did Jesus receive? What details does Mark provide?
4. With what crime did the leaders charge Jesus? How serious was the charge?

This chapter gives a detailed account of Jesus' trial, crucifixion, and death.

Since only the Romans could impose the death penalty, the Jewish leaders decided to take Jesus from their religious court to Pilate's civil court, probably about 6:00 A.M.

CHANGING COURTS AND CHARGES (15:1–5)

To the Roman government, the charge of blasphemy, which the Jews had pronounced, did not merit a death sentence from the civil court. So the Sanhedrin downplayed blasphemy and charged Jesus with treason.

When Pilate, the Roman governor, heard that Jesus was a Galilean, he sent Him to Herod Antipas, the Galilean ruler (Luke 23:5–12).

Actually, the accusing leaders made four specific charges against Jesus:

1. Stirring up people against Rome
2. Prohibiting the poll tax
3. Claiming to be a king
4. Claiming to be the Son of God (Luke 23:2; John 19:7).

The first two charges were false, and the last two charges were unrecognized truths about Jesus.

A CONDEMNING CROWD (15:6–15)

At Passover, it was customary for the Roman governor to release any *one* prisoner the people wanted released. When Pilate offered Jesus, the crowd instead chose Barabbas, a known murderer, thief, and insurrectionist. The crowd cried for crucifixion, and Pilate agreed to give them what they wanted. Pilate faced a dilemma. He wanted a clear conscience and at the same time he tried to appease the crowd.

Golgotha was the site of the crucifixion. It is an Aramaic word for "place of a skull." "Calvary" is the Latin translation of Golgotha, and it means a bare skull.

A REDEEMING DEATH (15:16–41)

After enduring cruel and brutal mockery, Jesus was crucified. Along with Jesus, two other men were crucified. They occupied the places that James and John had naively asked for (Mark 10:35–38).

Crucifixion was a cruel death on a cross. It involved the pain of a body torn by nails, exposure to the weather, and—if the person lasted long enough—hunger and thirst.

Unexplainable darkness came at noon and lasted until 3:00 P.M. Jesus cried out the words of Psalm 22:1, "Eloi, Eloi, lama sabachthani?" ("My God, my God, why have you forsaken me?") (v. 34). Some bystanders thought He was calling on Elijah to deliver Him from the cross (v. 35). Jesus then cried out and breathed His last.

At the moment Jesus died, the curtain of the Temple split from top to bottom (Mark 15:38; Matt. 27:51). There were two curtains or veils in the Temple: one at the entrance to the Temple itself and one that hung between the holy place and the Holy of Holies. If the curtain that split was the one that led to the Holy of Holies, it is symbolic of Jesus' gift of direct access to God. For up until that time only the high priest was to go into the Holy of Holies, and that was only on the Day of Atonement (see Lev. 16). Jesus provides direct access to God for every worshiper. If the curtain that split was the one at the entrance to the Temple, it foreshadows the destruction of the Temple. Either way, Jesus' death and the splitting of the curtain announced that things would never be the same again. There is a new day of faith and a new covenant!

BURYING THE MESSIAH (15:42–47)

Critical Timing (v. 42)

Jesus died about 3:00 P.M. on Friday afternoon, the day of preparation for the Sabbath. Because the Jewish Sabbath began at 6:00 P.M. on Friday evening, Jesus' burial presented a time problem for anyone who wanted to give Him a proper burial. Furthermore, touching a dead body made a Jew ceremonially unclean for seven days; so to bury Jesus on the Sabbath puts those friends of Jesus in a position of being unable to take part in the Sabbath or the religious festivities that would begin in a few hours.

Belated Bravery (v. 43–46)

Technically, Jesus' body belonged to the Roman government, as did the bodies of all executed criminals. The Romans usually left a body to decay on the cross unless friends or relatives asked for burial permission.

Joseph of Arimathea asked Pilate for the privilege of burying Jesus' body. When Pilate was convinced that Jesus was dead, he granted Jesus' body to Joseph for burial. Jesus was then laid in an unused tomb, which was sealed by a huge rock resembling a grindstone that is rolled downhill into its place at the entrance of the tomb.

Burdened Planning (v. 47)

Faithful women followed Jesus from the trial to Golgotha to the tomb. These women, with their deep love for Jesus, were still there when everyone else had gone. Mary Magdalene and Mary, the mother of Joses, watched to see where Jesus was buried.

Although the Romans had crucified Jesus, it was the Jews who had demanded the crucifixion. The Romans did not care how long a body hung on a cross. However, by Moses' Law, an executed criminal was not supposed to remain on a tree (or cross) overnight (Deut. 21:22–23). This explains why the Jewish leaders wanted to speed up the death of Jesus and the other two men on the crosses (John 19:31).

■ *Jesus was brought to Pilate the Roman governor, who reluctantly sentenced Him to death.*

QUESTIONS TO GUIDE YOUR STUDY

1. What were the charges against Jesus? How valid were they?
2. Did Jesus receive a fair trial? Describe Mark's account of the civil and legal proceedings.
3. The crowd chose to free Barabbas rather than Jesus. What was the cruel irony of their choice?
4. What is the significance of the rending of the curtain of the Temple?

HE IS RISEN! (16:1–8)

At sunrise, on the first day after the Sabbath, Mary Magdalene, Mary the mother of James, and Salome brought spices to annoint the body of Jesus. They were concerned because they did not know who would roll away the stone that guarded the tomb's entrance. The women were shocked to find the stone rolled away when they arrived. Inside was an angel who announced to the women the "He has risen!" The angel then commanded the women to tell the disciples about the resurrection. Terrified, the women fled, speaking to no one, "because they were afraid" (v. 8).

EPILOGUE (16:9–20)

"Afraid" (v. 8) does not appear to be a good word to end an account of good news, and though the oldest and best manuscripts do end with Mark 16:8, verses 9–20 and another ending began to show up very early in other manuscripts. Scholars differ on whether Mark intended to stop at 16:8, but they largely agree that what we have in 16:9–20 was not written by Mark. Five viewpoints summarize most thinking about the ending of the Gospel of Mark:

1. Mark completed his Gospel with 16:8 even though the ending is abrupt.
2. The original ending of Mark's Gospel may have been torn off at the end of the scroll.
3. Mark could have been interrupted and was not able to finish all he wanted to write in the inspired record.
4. Verses 9–20 are considered by some scholars to be a part of the original Mark's Gospel.

5. Verse 8 could have had a different ending as indicated in *The New English Bible*: "And they delivered all these instructions briefly to Peter and his companions. Afterwards Jesus himself sent out by them from east to west the sacred and imperishable message of eternal salvation."

Because we are almost two thousand years removed from the original writing, no one knows exactly how Mark ended his book. We do know that Jesus' tomb was empty and that Jesus appeared to His disciples on several occasions after His resurrection. Paul most concisely tells about resurrection appearances and the meaning of the whole Christ event (in 1 Cor. 15:3–8).

Paul's Account of Jesus' Post-Resurrection Appearances

Appearance	Passage
1. Peter	Luke 24:34; Mark 16:7; John 21:1–14
2. The Eleven	Matt. 28:16–20; Luke 24:36–49; John 20:19–25
3. Five hundred believers	1 Cor. 15:6
4. James	1 Cor. 15:7
5. The apostles	1 Cor. 15:7
6. Paul	1 Cor. 15:8

Regardless of whether the verses originally appeared in the Gospel of Mark, it is still important to take a summary look at Mark 16:9–20. Most of the content in these verses appears elsewhere in the Gospels or in Acts. The breakdown of verses 9–20 and their possible counterparts elsewhere may be helpful:

- *Verses 9–11:* Appearance to Mary Magdalene (see Luke 24:10–11, 22–24; John 20:11–18; and possibly John 20:1–2).
- *Verses 12–13:* Appearance to the two travelers (see Luke 24:13–35).
- *Verses 14–18:* Appearance to the Eleven (see Luke 24:36–49; Matt. 28:16–20; and parts of the book of Acts).
- *Verses 19–20:* Ascension and continued activity (see Acts 1:9–11).

Scholars see other parallels in addition to these, but the heart of Mark 16:9–20 is reflected in the passages cited above. Readers will share different concerns about the verses that likely were not in Mark's original Gospel and which may not have support elsewhere in the New Testament. For example, with regard to drinking something deadly or picking up serpents (v. 18), it does not seem wise to build a theological position on these verses alone.

Verses 9–20 call Christians to preach and minister in the power of the resurrected Christ, who did not leave His disciples alone to continue His work.

We now come to the end of Mark's record about Jesus. But the end of that story is only a beginning for those who turn from their sin and put their trust in Jesus as Lord and Savior. Mark's Gospel is not a biography. It is good news that calls for every person to decide what he or she will do personally with Jesus Christ. The essential truth is this: *Jesus Christ is God's good news for mankind, and Jesus alone is the way to eternal life.* Outside of Christ there is only spiritual death. So life's crucial question to all who read this Gospel is: What will you do with Jesus?

- *Mary Magdalene, Mary, mother of James,*
- *and Salome came to the tomb to anoint the*
- *body of Jesus. They found the tomb empty*
- *and a young man who told them that Jesus*
- *had risen from the grave. The messenger told*
- *the women to tell this to the disciples, who*
- *were to go to Galilee where Jesus would meet*
- *them.*

QUESTIONS TO GUIDE YOUR STUDY

1. When the women arrived at the tomb, what were they expecting to see? Describe what happened.
2. What makes the resurrection so important to the Christian faith?
3. What does the resurrection of Jesus mean to you?
4. Why are verses 9–20 of Mark 16 controversial? How is this passage viewed by most believers? What is your view?
5. How would you summarize the importance of Mark's Gospel to your understanding and Christian experience?

LIST OF REFERENCE SOURCES USED

The following list is a collection of the sources used for this volume. All are from Broadman & Holman's list of published reference resources. They are designed to accommodate the reader's need for more specific information and for an expanded treatment of the Gospel of Mark. All of these works will greatly aid in the reader's study, teaching, and presentation of the message of Mark's Gospel. The accompanying annotations can be helpful in guiding the reader to the proper resources.

Adams, J. McKee, rev. By Joseph A. Callaway, *Biblical Backgrounds*. This work provides valuable information on the physical and geographical settings of the New Testament. Its many color maps and other features add depth and understanding.

Blair, Joe, *Introducing the New Testament*, pp. 71–80. Designed as a core textbook for New Testament survey courses, this volume helps the reader in understanding the content and principles of the New Testament. Its features include special maps and photos, outlines, and discussion questions.

Brooks, James A., *Mark* (The New American Commentary, Vol . 23). A theological commentary on Mark.

Cate, Robert L., *A History of the New Testament and Its Times*. An excellent and thorough survey of the birth and growth of the Christian faith in the first-century world.

Godwin, Johnnie C., *Mark* (Layman's Bible Book Commentary, Vol. 16). A popular-level treatment of Mark. This easy-to-use volume provides a relevant and practical perspective for the reader.

Holman Bible Dictionary. An exhaustive, alphabetically arranged resource of Bible-related subjects. An excellent tool of definitions and other information on the people, places, things, and events of the Bible.

Holman Bible Handbook, pp. 568–584. A comprehensive treatment that offers outlines, commentary on key themes and sections, and full-color photos, illustrations, charts, and maps. Provides an accent on the broader theological teachings of the Gospel of Mark.

Holman Book of Biblical Charts, Maps, and Reconstructions. A colorful, visual collection of charts, maps, and reconstructions, these well-designed tools are invaluable to the study of the Bible.

Robertson, A. T., *Word Pictures in the New Testament,* "Matthew and Mark" Vol. 1. This six-volume series provides insights into the language of the New Testament—Greek. Provides word studies as well as grammatical and background insights into Mark's Gospel.

Controversy Stories in Mark

CONTROVERSY	REFERENCE IN MARK
Over Jesus' right to forgive sins	2:1–12
Over Jesus' fellowship with tax collectors and "sinners"	2:13–17
Over the disciples' freedom from fasting	2:18–22
Over the disciples' picking grain on the Sabbath	2:23–27
Over Jesus' right to do good on the Sabbath	3:1–6
Over the nature of Jesus' family	3:20–21,31–35
Over the source of Jesus' power to exorcise	3:22–30
Over the disciples' eating with unwashed hands	7:1–5,14–23
Over the Pharisees' and teachers' of the law setting aside the commands of God in order to observe their own tradition	7:6–13
Over the legality of divorce and God's intention for marriage	10:1–12
Over Jesus' authority to cleanse the temple and John's authority to baptize	11:27–33
Over paying taxes to Caesar and giving God His due	12:13–17
Over marriage at the resurrection, the power of God, and the witness of Scripture	12:18–27
Over the most important commandment	12:28–34
Over the nature of the Messiah—son of David or David's Lord	12:35–37

Harmony of the Gospels

	MATT.	MARK	LUKE	JOHN
PART I. INTRODUCTORY STATEMENTS				
1. Luke's Historical Introduction			1:1–4	
2. John's Theological Introduction				1:1–18
3. Matthew's and Luke's Genealogical Introductions	1:1–17		3:23–58	
PART II. THE BIRTH AND YOUTH OF JOHN THE BAPTIST AND JESUS				
4. The Annunciation to Zacharias Place: Jerusalem			1:5–25	
5. The Annunciation to the Virgin Mary Place: Nazareth			1:26–38	
6. Songs of Elizabeth and Mary Place: Judea			1:39–56	
7. Birth and Youth of John the Baptist Place: Judea			1:57–80	
8. The Annunciation to Joseph Place: Nazareth	1:18–25			
9. The Birth of Jesus Place: Bethlehem			2:1–7	
10. The Angel and Shepherds Place: Near Bethlehem			2:8–20	
11. Circumcision and Naming of Jesus Place: Bethlehem			2:21	
12. The Presentation in the Temple Place: Jerusalem			2:22–38	

Harmony of the Gospels

	MATT.	MARK	LUKE	JOHN
13. The Visit of the Wise Men Places: Jerusalem, Bethlehem	2:1–12			
14. Flight to Egypt and Return to Nazareth Places: Nazareth, Egypt	2:13–23		2:39	
15. His Youth in Nazareth and Visit to Jerusalem Places: Nazareth, Jerusalem			2:40–52	
PART III. MINISTRY OF JOHN THE BAPTIST				
16. The Coming of the Word Place: Wilderness		1:1	3:1–2	
17. Response of John in the Wilderness Place: Wilderness	3:1–6	1:26	3:3–6	
18. The Boldness of His Preaching Place: Wilderness	3:7–10		3:7–14	
19. John's Idea of the Messiah	3:11, 12	1:7, 8	3:15–18	
PART IV. EARLY MINISTRY OF JESUS				
20. The Baptism in the Jordan Place: Jordan	3:13–17	1:9–11	3:21–23	
21. The Temptation of Jesus by Satan Place: Judean Wilderness	4:1–11	1:12, 13	4: 1–13	
22. Testimony of John and Disciples Place: Bethany				1: 19–51

Harmony of the Gospels

	MATT.	MARK	LUKE	JOHN
23. The First Miracle Place: Cana				2:1–11
24. The First Stay in Capernaum Place: Capernaum				2:12
25. First Passover and Cleansing of Temple Place: Jerusalem				2:13–3:21
26. Closing Ministry and Arrest of John Place: Aenon			3:19, 20	4:1–3
27. Jesus at Jacob's Well and Sychar Place: Samaria				4:4–42
28. Jesus Returns to Galilee Place: Galilee	4:12	1:14	4:14	4:43–45
PART V. THE MINISTRY IN GALILEE				
29. The Message of Jesus—Repentance Place: Galilee	4:17	1:14–15	4:14–15	
30. Healing the Centurion's Son Place: Capernaum				4:46–54
31. Jesus Rejected by the People Place: Nazareth	4:13–16		4:16–31	
32. Calling the Four Fishermen Place: Capernaum	4:18–22	1:16–20	5:1–11	
33. A Busy Sabbath in Capernaum Place: Capernaum	8:14–17	1:21–34	4:32–41	
34. The First Tour of Galilee Place: Galilee	4:23–25	1:35–39	4:42–44	

Harmony of the Gospels

	MATT.	MARK	LUKE	JOHN
35. The Healing of a Leper Place: Galilee	8:2–4	1:40–45	5:12–16	
36. Healing the Paralytic in Peter's Home Place: Capernaum	9:1–8	2:1–2	5:17–26	
37. The Call of Matthew (Levi) Place: Sea of Galilee	9:9–13	2:13–17	5:27–32	
38. Three Parables About Fasting Place: The Seaside	9:14–17	2:18–22	5:33–39	
39. First Sabbath Controversy in Jerusalem Place: Jerusalem				5:1–47
40. Further Controversies in Galilee Place: Galilee	12:1–14	2:23–3:6	6:1–11	
41. Choosing the Twelve and Sermon on the Mount Place: Near Capernaum	10:1–5;5:1–8:1	3:14–19	6:12–49	
42. Healing the Centurion's Servant Place: Capernaum	8:5–13		7:1–10	
43. Raising the Son of a Widow Place: Nain			7:11–17	
44. Doubt of John and Praise of Jesus Place: Nain	11:2–19		7:18–35	
45. The Cities of Opportunity Place: Capernaum	11:20–30			

Harmony of the Gospels

	MATT.	MARK	LUKE	JOHN
46. The Sinful Woman in House of Simon Place: Capernaum			7:36–50	
47. Jesus and Disciples Go to Galilee			8:1–3	
48. Jesus Accused of Blasphemy Place: Galilee	12:15–45	3:19–30		
49. The Mother of Jesus Calls Him	12:46–50	3:31–35	8:19–21	
50. The First Extended Group of Parables Place: Sea of Galilee	13:1–53	4:1–34	8:4–18	
51. Jesus Stills the Storm and Heals Demoniac Places: Sea of Galilee; Gadara	8:23–34	4:35–5:20	8:22–39	
52. Healing Jairus' Daughter and Woman with Issue of Blood Place: Capernaum	9:18–26	5:21–43	8:40–56	
53. Two Blind Men and Demoniac Healed Place: Capernaum	9:27–34			
54. Last Rejection at Nazareth Place: Nazareth	13:54–58	6:1–6		
55. The Disciples Given Power to Heal Place: Capernaum	10:1–42	6:7–13	9:1–6	
56. Herod Fears John and Jesus	14:1–12	6:14–29	9:7–9	

Harmony of the Gospels

	MATT.	MARK	LUKE	JOHN
PART VI. THE WITHDRAWAL FROM GALILEE				
57. First Withdrawal to Bethsaida-Julias	14:13–21	6:30–44	9:10–17	6:1–13
58. The Return to Gennesaret Place: Lake of Gennesaret	14:22–36	6:45–56		6:14–21
59. Rejection of Christ in the Synagogue Place: Capernaum				6:22–71
60. Criticism of the Pharisees Concerning Unwashed Hands Place: Capernaum	15:1–20	7:1–23		7:1
61. Healing Daughter of Syrophoenecian Place: Phoenicia	15:21–28	7:24–30		
62. Jesus Departs to Sea of Galilee	15:29–38	7:31–8:9		
63. Pharisees and Sadducees Attack Jesus, Again Asking a Sign Place: Dalmanutha or Magadan	15:39–16:4	8:10–12		
64. Jesus Again Withdraws to Bethsaida-Julias Place: Bethsaida	16:5–12	8:13–26		
65. The Great Confession of Peter Place: Caesarea-Philippi	16:13–20	8:27–30	9:18–21	

Harmony of the Gospels

	MATT.	MARK	LUKE	JOHN
66. Jesus Predicts His Death and Resurrection Place: Galilee	16:21–28	8:31–38; 9:1	9:22–27	
67. The Transfiguration of Jesus Place: Mt. Tabor	17:1–13	9:2–13	9:28–36	
68. Disciples Unable to Cast Out Evil Spirit	17:14–21	9:14–29	9:37–42	
69. Further Reference to His Death and Resurrection Place: Galilee	17:22–23	9:30–32	9:42–45	
70. Jesus Pays Tax by Miracle Place: Capernaum	17:24–27			
71. Disciples Contending Who Is Greatest Place: Capernaum	18:1–5	9:33–37	9:46–48	
72. Jesus Rebukes the Narrowness of John Place: Capernaum	18:6–14	9:38–50	9:49–50	
73. On Forgiving a Brother Place: Capernaum	18:15–35			
74. Christ Requires Full Consecration Place: Capernaum	8:19–22		9:57–62	
75. His Unbelieving Brethren Rebuked Place: Capernaum				7:2–10
76. James and John Rebuked for Anger Place: Samaria			9:51–56	

Harmony of the Gospels

	MATT.	MARK	LUKE	JOHN
PART VII. THE MINISTRY IN JUDEA				
77. At the Feast of Tabernacles Place: Jerusalem				7:11–8:11
78. Jesus the Light of the World Place: Jerusalem				8:12–59
79. Opened Eyes of Man Born Blind Place: Jerusalem				9:1–41
80. Parable of the Good Shepherd Place: Jerusalem				10:1–21
81. The Seventy Sent Out			10:1–24	
82. Parable of the Good Samaritan Place: Jerusalem			10:25–37	
83. Jesus Received by Martha and Mary Place: Bethany			10:38–42	
84. The Disciples Taught How to Pray	6:9–13		11:1–13	
85. Accused of Healing Through Beelzebub			11:14–36	
86. The Criticism of Pharisee and Lawyer			11:37–54	
87. Warning the Disciples Against the Leaven of the Pharisees			12:1–12	
88. Covetousness and Parable of Rich Man			12:13–21	
89. The Ravens and Lilies			12:22–34	

Harmony of the Gospels

	MATT.	MARK	LUKE	JOHN
90. The Second Coming Referred to by Jesus.			12:35–48	
91. Christ's Eagerness for His Baptism of Death on the Cross			12:49–59	
92. Repentance and Parable of Fig Tree			13:1–9	
93. The Infirm Woman Healed on Sabbath			13:10–21	
94. Jesus at Feast of Dedication Place: Jerusalem				10:22–39
PART VIII. THE MINISTRY IN PEREA				
95. Many Believe on Jesus Place: Bethany				10:40–42
96. Asked Concerning Number of the Saved Place: Perea			13:22–35	
97. Jesus Teaches Humility and Service Place: Near Jerusalem			14:1–24	
98. To Be Christ's Disciple Requires Forsaking All Place: Jerusalem			14:25–35	
99. Christ Justifies Himself in Receiving Sinners			15:1–32	
100. Parables Concerning Stewardship			16:1–17:10	

Harmony of the Gospels

	MATT.	MARK	LUKE	JOHN
101. The Raising of Lazarus Place: Bethany				11:1–54
102. Jesus Goes to Jerusalem for the Passover Places: Samaria, Galilee			17:11–37	
103. Parables on Prayer on Way to Jerusalem	19:1–2	10:1	18:1–14	
104. Pharisees Tempt Jesus Concerning Divorce	19:3–12	10:2–12		
105. Christ Welcomes Little Children Place: Perea	19:13–15	10:13–16	18:15–17	
106. Parable of the Rich Young Ruler	19:16–29	10:17–30	18:18–30	
107. Parable of the Laborers in Vineyard	20:1–16	10:31		
108. Jesus Again Refers to Death and Resurrection	20:17–19	10:32–34	18:31–34	
109. Selfishness of James and John	20:20–28	10:35–45		
110. Blind Bartimaeus Receives His Sight	20:29–34	10:46–52	18:35–43	
111. Zaccheus and Parable of the Pounds Place: Jericho			19:1–28	
PART IX. THE LAST JERUSALEM MINISTRY				
112. The Interest in Jesus and Lazarus Place: Bethany				11:55–57; 12:1, 9–11

Harmony of the Gospels

	MATT.	MARK	LUKE	JOHN
113. The Challenge to the Sanhedrin Place: Jerusalem	21:1–17	11:1–11	19:29–44	12:12–19
114. Cursing the Fig Tree—Cleansing Temple Place: Jerusalem	21:18–19, 12–13	11:12–18	19:45–48	
115. The Greeks Seek Jesus While He Is in Agony of Soul Place: Jerusalem				12:20–50
116. The Withered Fig Tree, and the Power of Faith Place: Jerusalem	21:19–22	11:19–26	21:37–38	
117.Sanhedrin Questions the Authority of Jesus Place: Jerusalem	21:23–46; 22:1–14	11:27–12:12	20:1–19	
118. An Attempt to Trap Jesus Concerning Tribute to Caesar Place: Jerusalem	22:15–22	12:13–17	20:20–26	
119. A Further Attempt to Confuse Jesus Place: Jerusalem	22:23–33	12:18–27	20:27–40	
120. The Legal Problem of a Lawyer Place: Jerusalem	22:34–40	12:28–34		
121. Jesus Silences Enemies by Appeal to David Place: Jerusalem	22:41–46	12:35–37	20:41–44	

Harmony of the Gospels

	Matt.	Mark	Luke	John
122. A Denunciation of Scribes and Pharisees Place: Jerusalem	23:1–39	12:38–40	20:45–47	
123. The Widow's Two Mites Place: Jerusalem		12:41–44	21:1–4	
PART X. JESUS COUNSELS HIS DISCIPLES LEADING UP TO HIS SACRIFICE				
124. The Great Eschatological Discourse Place: Jerusalem	24:1–25:46	13:1–37	21:5–36	
125. Jesus Predicts His Arrest Place: Jerusalem	26:1–5	14:1–2	22:1–2	
126. Jesus Anointed by Mary Place: Bethany	26:6–13	14:3–9		12:2–8
127. The Act of Judas Iscariot Place: Jerusalem	26:14–16	14:10–11	22:3–6	
128. Preparation for Passover and Jealousy of the Disciples Place: Jerusalem	26:17–20	14:12–17	22:7–16, 24–30	
129. Jesus Washes the Apostles' Feet Place: Jerusalem				13:1–20
130. Judas Named as the Betrayer Place: Jerusalem	26:21–25	14:18–21	22:21–23	13:21–30
131. Steadfastness of the Disciples Questioned Place: Jerusalem	26:31–35	14:27–31	22:17–20	13:34–38

Harmony of the Gospels

	MATT.	MARK	LUKE	JOHN
132. The Memorial Supper Instituted Place: Jerusalem	26:26–29	14:22–25	22:17–20	(See 1 Cor. 11:23–26)
133. Jesus Opens His Heart to the Disciples Concerning His Departure Place: Upper Room and on Way to Gethsemane				14:1–16:33
134. The Intercessory Prayer Place: Near Gethsemane				17:1–26
135. The Agony in Gethsemane	26:36–46	14:32–42	22:39–46	18:1
PART XI. THE CONDEMNATION AND THE CROSS				
136. The Betrayal, Arrest, and Desertion by the Disciples Place: Gethsemane	26:47–56	14:43–52	22:47–53	18:2–12
137. The Examination by Annas Place: Jerusalem				18:13–14, 19–23
138. Condemned on Perjured Testimony Place: Jerusalem	26:57–68	14:53–65	22:54, 63–65	18:24
139. Peter's Three Denials Place: Jerusalem	26:58, 69–75	14:54, 66–72	22:54–62	18:15–18, 25–27
140. An Attempt to Make the Trial Legal Place: Jerusalem	27:1	15:1	22:66–71	

Harmony of the Gospels

	MATT.	MARK	LUKE	JOHN
141. Judas Realizes His Sin Place: Jerusalem	27:3–10		(See Acts 1:18–19)	
142. Jesus Before Pilate Place: Jerusalem	27:2, 11–14	15:2–5	23:1–5	18:28–38
143. Jesus Is Sent to Herod Place: Jerusalem			23:6–12	
144. Herod Returns Jesus to Pilate Place: Jerusalem	27:15–26	15:6–15	23:13–25	18:39–19:16
145.Jesus Is Mocked by Soldiers Place: Jerusalem	27:27–30	15:16–19		
146. Simon Bears the Cross Place: On Way to Calvary	27:31–34	15:20–23	23:26–33	19:16–17
147. Jesus Is Crucified Place: Calvary	27:95–50	15:24–37	23:33–46	19:18–30
148. The Supernatural Phenomena Place: Jerusalem	27:51–56	15:38–41	23:45–49	
149.Burial in Joseph's Tomb Place: Gethsemane	27:57–60	15:42–46	23:50–54	19:31–42
150.The Women by the Sepulcher	27:61–66	15:47	23:55–56	
PART XII. THE RESURRECTION AND ASCENSION				
151. At the Tomb on the Sabbath Place: Gethsemane	28:1			
152. Anointing with Spices		16:1		
153. The Tomb Is Opened	28:2–4			

Harmony of the Gospels

	MATT.	MARK	LUKE	JOHN
154. Women Find the Empty Tomb and Angels	28:5–8	16:2–8	24:1–8	20:1
155. The Women Report to the Apostles Place: Jerusalem			24:9–12	20:2–10
156. Jesus Appears to Mary Magdalene Place: Jerusalem		16:9–11		20:11–18
157. Then Other Women See Him	28:9–10			
158. The Watchmen Bribed to Claim the Body Taken by the Disciples	28:11–15			
159. Jesus Appears on Way to Emmaus		16:12–13	24:13–32	
160. Simon Peter Sees Jesus			24:33–35	(see also 1 Cor. 15:5)
161. Entire Group, Except Thomas, See Him, and He Eats Before Them Place: Jerusalem		16:14	24:36–43	20:19–25
162. Entire Group, with Thomas, See Him, Finally Believing				20:26–31
163. Jesus Appears by Sea of Galilee				21:1–25
164. The Apostles Commissioned to Preach Place: Galilee	28:16–20	16:15–18	(see also 1 Cor. 15:6)	

Harmony of the Gospels

	MATT.	MARK	LUKE	JOHN
165. James the Brother of Jesus Sees Him			1 Cor. 15:7)	
166. Jesus and Disciples Counsel for the Last Time and Jesus Ascends Place: Olivet		16:19–20	24:44–53	(see also Acts 1:3–12)